Death to the Death of Poetry

POETS ON POETRY · Donald Hall, General Editor

Donald Hall

Death to the Death of Poetry

ESSAYS, REVIEWS, NOTES, INTERVIEWS

Ann Arbor

THE UNIVERSITY OF MICHIGAN PRESS

Copyright © by the University of Michigan 1994
All rights reserved
Published in the United States of America by
The University of Michigan Press
Manufactured in the United States of America
⊗Printed on acid-free paper

1997 1996 1995 1994   4 3 2 1

A CIP catalogue record for this book is available from the British Library.

Library of Congress Cataloging-in-Publication Data

Hall, Donald, 1928–
    Death to the death of poetry: essays, reviews, notes, interviews
/ Donald Hall.
        p.   cm.—(Poets on poetry)
Includes bibliographical references and index.
ISBN 0-472-09571-4 (alk. paper).—ISBN 0-472-06571-8 (pbk.:
alk. paper)
        1. Hall, Donald, 1928–   —Interviews. 2. American poetry—20th
century—History and criticism—Theory, etc. 3. Poets,
American—20th century—Interviews. 4. Poetry—Book reviews.
5. Poetry—Authorship.   I. Title.   II. Series.
PS3515.A31Z463   1994
811'.5409—dc20   94-27082
                                                            CIP

for Linda Zuckerman

Contents

Note

My title refers to poetry's obituary notice, running daily in your local paper. Most elegists, as I remark, believe that they love poetry—and mope over its decline while it gambols around them. People conscious that they loathe poetry seldom take the time to announce their antipathy, but it is prudent to remember how many Americans—in sincere passion, with true feeling—despise this art that some of us live by. After all, we inhabit a country founded, by forefathers other than Thomas Jefferson, on contempt for art and artists: see Tocqueville *passim;* see the *Congressional Record.* When we hear notice of "the American dream," we hear about prospects for comfort and prosperity, bless them, and not about beauty, imagination, spirit, mind, or pleasure. Diatribes from our current art-bashers—columnists, senators, fundamentalists—bring nothing new to our culture. America's eminent know-nothings have always understood: *Artists are sissies providing pastimes for rich folks.* Thus a merchant of popular science, writing in the *New York Times Book Review,* deplores the "routinely flowery tradition in poetry," and suggests removing great poetry from Bartlett's—removing Marvell, removing Pound—to substitute "Here's Johnny," Dr. Seuss, "Beam me up, Scotty," and "the poetry of physics." When we hear about the *poetry* of golf or direct-mail advertising or hair implants, we hear someone who cannot distinguish poems from solid waste.

Initial Education

Writing poems for fifty years, I've altered as much in the last twenty-five as I did in the first. Education doesn't stop—or it better hadn't. In my latest quarter-century, a first marriage ended; a second marriage, to a poet, has supplied twenty years of instruction—among other pleasures. Early in this period, I spent six years in psychotherapy with an analyst. It was only seventeen years ago that I left the academy to freelance on a family place in New Hampshire. My reading has become eclectic; finding Gibbon, a dozen years ago, has been crucial to late education. Yet, despite Gibbon, I've become Christian. In my fifties and sixties, I've been educated by friendship and correspondence with poets twenty and thirty years younger. When I was twenty I looked on education as terminal; after a while, you knew or you didn't know. But knowing prevents learning. When developmental phases stop and you are at last complete, you are dead.

Tonight I want to talk about early education, even education before education. Because I've addressed these matters piecemeal before, I must in part repeat myself.

Is there a propensity toward poetry in an infant, even before the infant speaks? When Freud wrote about the relationship of the writer to daydream, he treated plots as wish fulfillment—and a story's content derived its manifest from the covert. Then, in one quick hit, Freud said that he would not discuss the provenance of literary form but that he be-

---

The Academy of American Poets sponsors an annual lecture on the "Education of a Poet." It was my turn to deliver the lecture, later reprinted in *Poetry Pilot,* in 1991.

lieved it was related to forepleasure. The remark is mysterious but I believe its suggestion correct. Poetry is more erotic than prose and its eroticism begins long before we approach a poem's statement. A poem can tell us that leaves fall in the autumn but come back in the spring; it can tell us that children are dear but that they grow old and die—things we never knew before—but if it is beautiful poetry, when we read it or hear it our skin tingles and our eyes glisten; we are aroused. It used to strike me as curious that, in the nineteenth century, a masculine literary culture allowed women to write great fiction but not great poetry. When a woman like Emily Dickinson wrote dazzling poems, men became nervous: Poetry was too openly sexual—and Victorian women avoided short skirts.

When my children were tiny I loved the sounds they made in their cribs, happy in the morning. This cooing is autistic utterance, and it is the beginning of poetry: pleasure in the mouth, lips and tongues rubbing together to make sound without meaning. While the mouth nibbles on noises, the same infant pulses its limbs rhythmically. Limb-motion is rhythm or dance, sound in the shape of leg-pleasure that joins the mouth-joy of autistic utterance. Here is the beginning of delight in sensuous sound, before words come; here is the beginning of poetry.

Oh, I'll admit that the six months child does not write "Out of the Cradle" or "An Horatian Ode upon Cromwell's Return from Ireland." Education has a distance to travel; but the crib is where poetry starts—and the poet is a grown-up who never wholly abandons crib-pleasure. If the adult is to write poetry, the adult must add complexities of syntax and lexicon as well as intelligence in the service of emotional ambivalence learned in bliss and betrayal. But if crib-pleasure does not endure, there will be no poetry.

Why does one person preserve the infant's bodily joy into forms of adulthood and another not? Perhaps the source is partly genetic. But we can speculate only about a *behavioral* etiology.

Where I grew up in the Connecticut suburbs, my silent grandfather Henry loved songs and horses but not speech.

Maybe his wife provided me indirect help; my grandmother Augusta was the child of parents who spoke English with an accent, and she took care to speak *correctly;* over-attention to niceties of speech is at least attention. My father, who was their child, cared little for beauty of language but was a stickler for purity of diction. Growing up, I heard him ridicule the jargon of the business world in which he made his living. When he erred in style, it was on the side of a precise polysyllabic pomposity, especially when depressed: I remember him sitting, melancholy at the supper table, watching me eat too fast, saying, "It is necessary to masticate thoroughly." On the other hand, my mother connected me to lyric poetry; she recited poems or read them aloud from a wonderful anthology called *Silver Pennies,* performing dramatically or poetically, never trying to sound merely natural. In that book she discovered the favorite poem of my infancy: Vachel Lindsay's verses in which the moon is the north wind's cookie. (No one who has read my things will be surprised that my favorite poem was about eating.) My father was a critic nodding his negative head, my mother a breeze enhancing the spirited wind—and *no* is as requisite as *yes.*

In my childhood, I cherished an alternative to the business-like suburbs—and it was the rural New Hampshire where my mother's people lived. For my mother, suburban Connecticut was exile that she embraced as the Modern World. But I chose the mother's origin over the father's—oh, unprecedented act for the infant male poet!—preferring New Hampshire to Connecticut, the rundown farmhouse to the six-room suburban nest, outhouse to white-tiled bathroom, old horse and shabby buggy to the Studebaker bought new every two years.

New Hampshire I visited frequently, often without my parents, and it became the place of poetry. My grandmother Kate had memorized hundreds of lines as a child, which she recited in singsong. As I walked into the kitchen from the barnyard, she would turn from the stove, raise her hands holding a spatula or a rolling pin, and recite: "Blessings on thee, little man, / Barefoot boy, with cheek of tan!" My farmer grandfather Wesley spoke poems aloud that he learned when he was young, to entertain or compete in Lyceums. He knew hundreds word for word and recited them while he milked cows in the tie-up, keeping time with the alternate streams of milk, or as we sat in the hayrack pulled by Riley on our way to the hayfield. The poems that he recited reached the literary heights of "Casey at the Bat." I remember one about "Lawyer Green," born with green skin, ridiculed in his town, who went to the city, became rich and famous as a lawyer, and returned to his town—which now found him acceptable; or a poem about the hypocrisy of the Squire (that was the word) who looked pious at church but drank rum in secret. They were bouncy, enthusiastic poems, righteous and funny and populist, without beauty of sound or metaphor but with the wit of rhyming and of the smart answer, with pointed and deliberate language for the goal of amusement and righteous common sense affirmed together.

Not only was poetry a portion of social life; social life in this universe was narrative: church with its stories of Joseph and of the Prodigal Son, and Old Home Day with its reminiscence—as Ulysses returned annually to Ithaca, to dog and nursemaid. Neighbors and cousins came calling on Sunday afternoons to sit and tell stories; I talked with an old man who remembered the Civil War. Country people were storytellers—they still are—with a notion not only of narrative but of language directed toward closure, resolution by plot and style. I studied in a geriatric school.

These backgrounds to poetry remained in place as other ingredients accumulated—ingredients distant from the tie-up and "Lawyer Green." When I was eleven or twelve, I felt the access of ambition; I mean ambition wholly generic, with no direction except whim. Would I be a movie star? Would I be president of the United States? Would I be a millionaire or a famous criminal? It didn't matter what path I chose; what mattered was eminence or notoriety. (Oliver Wendell Holmes said that nothing is so commonplace as the desire to be extraordinary.) An only grandchild on both sides, I was aware that I carried my family on my shoulders; mostly I enjoyed the burden. Precocious reading was one result of ambition, and at eleven or twelve I leapt from Albert Payson Terhune to Gustave Flaubert out of the wish to be considered intelligent or precocious—or possibly out of the desire to terrify parents and teachers.

Another ingredient, in this poetry goulash, was my morbidity, which started early. On my ninth birthday, shortly after the death of a great-aunt, I lay in bed thinking about my own death, repeating to myself, "Now death has become a reality." It was as if I were writing a biography: "When Donald Hall turned nine, death became a reality." At my great-aunt's funeral, my Uncle George had a pain in his back: I attended his funeral four or five months later. My grandparents' siblings, on both sides, were older than my grandparents, lived to considerable ages, and one by one expired. Then a young male cousin, only a little older than I was, died of pneumonia. Were these deaths a source of my morbidity? Maybe, but I am skeptical; I suspect my morbidity started earlier from a requirement to suppress erotic feeling, especially for my mother; I needed to frighten myself with Omega in order not to recognize Alpha. At the age of twelve I bused downtown from our suburb Saturday afternoons to watch horror movies—various incarnations of the Wolf Man and Frankenstein's monster . . . The boy next door told me: If you like that stuff, you ought to read Edgar Allan Poe.

From that moment my life-as-it-is began. I *adored* Poe, both stories and poems. At twelve I wrote my first poem, imitating not Poe's prosody but his morbidity, which licensed my own. Hervey Allen, my father's favorite historical novelist, had written a biography of Poe called *Israfel*. Reading it when I was twelve, out of love for Poe, I fattened on *le poète maudit:* I would model my life on Poe's. Allen remarked that Poe read Keats and Shelley when he was fourteen. I had never heard of Keats and Shelley, so I bought the Modern Library Giant *Keats and Shelley* in order to be two years better than my master. Thereupon I wrote sonnets under the influence of the Romantic early nineteenth century. When I was fourteen I met a sixteen-year-old who dazzled me by affirming that his profession was poetry; he had just quit school in order to write poetry full time. And *he* knew freshmen at Yale, eighteen years old, who read T. S. Eliot.

For several years in my middle teens I flitted from poet to poet in a mad sequence of enthusiasms, falling in love with one and then another—giddy, ecstatic, and faithless. My first was H.D., a fortunate fall. These were early imagistic pieces like "Heat," poems an adolescent could learn from: no intellectual or syntactic complexity, little allusion, but abundant erotic form. After her, I ran through a rapid sequence of infatuations, all with moderns: Eliot, Cummings, Stevens, Yeats, Moore, Williams, Crane. Sometimes I loved a poet because I admired misery, madness, and suicide; Untermeyer's headnotes were romantic enough, and it was his suicide that brought me to Hart Crane. But I must add: it wasn't his suicide that kept me reading Hart Crane, and keeps me reading him still. After coming to poetry for reasons of morbidity and romance—or to interest the cheerleaders—I came to love the *art,* not merely myself as potential artist. I came to love poems for their own beautiful sakes.

When I was sixteen I first published in magazines—country poems in *Trails,* modernist endeavors in *Matrix* and *Experiment*—signing them "Don A. Hall." Although I wrote about scythe-mowing (and read Frost) I also wrote something like surrealism, having gloried in James Laughlin's *New Directions* annuals. Not long ago an old schoolmate sent me a typescript of a poem called "Cain," which I wrote at sixteen. It ends:

> Bits of wood smoulder; the ice itself
> is in flames; the flesh drains back into the earth
> and into flesh again; mud bubbles up through the ground
> and old roots feel new life; man himself stretches
> and yawns and laughs at his face in the mirror.
> New blood mounts in all their crusted veins.
>
> *They grasp at their senses like well-worn clothes.*

I wrote this poem at Exeter, where I studied for two years after two years of Hamden High School. Prep school was hard and therefore useful. Although I was never good at Latin or Greek, studies in these languages helped educate me. Two Exeter teachers loved modern poetry and I cherished their companionship and support, but most of my English teachers considered modern poetry a fraud. (This error did not keep them from teaching Macbeth or Melville with close attention to language.) One teacher made it his public purpose to get me to stop writing poetry—because it wasted time I might have spent on studies. Rebelling against him was energizing; it was probably also self-deceiving, because although I thought I rebelled, I also kowtowed. It was at Exeter (after "Cain") that I began to write metrical poetry. I don't regret that apprenticeship; I spent ten years writing in meter, obsessed with prosody and learning things I haven't forgotten. At Oxford I wrote a B.Litt. thesis: "Eighteenth Century Prosodists, with Especial Attention to Bysshe and Steele."

Of course there's more to tell, including my two weeks as a Contributor at Bread Loaf when I was sixteen in 1945. I met Robert Frost, I drank bourbon . . . Two years later I went to college, which was easy because prep school had been difficult. In Harvard's Poetry Room I spent four years listening to poets speak their poems on unique discs. My classes in literature were rigorous, and I had the stimulus of tutorial with Harry Levin—as gentle as he was terrifying. I read the old poets, concentrating on the seventeenth century. But mostly I devoted myself to conversation and competition, for nothing in schoolwork was so exciting as the other students: Robert Bly, Adrienne Rich, John Ashbery, Frank O'Hara, Peter Davison, L. E. Sissman, Harold Brodkey, and Kenneth Koch.

Of course, none of us undergraduates knew that we would ever publish—except that Adrienne was Yale Younger Poet when she and I were seniors. It was a heady time. Recently I found an *Advocate* for September, 1948, including an unsigned, very sophisticated (E. B. Whitened) piece of chat beginning "Harvard is a guppy that eats its own young . . ."—and I can reveal that its author was the literary editor, then known as Robert E. Bly. In the same issue is a page-long poem by John Ashbery, a short story by one Francis O'Hara, and "In Dream and Asylums" by Donald A. Hall:

> In dreams and asylums there is no arithmetic.
> Unreasoned progression belongs to the child, whose clocks

Gossip on mantles, appear without faces in sleep;
Whose three o'clock is the forest of the sun,
Where corridors of musk lead down the earth
To a minimum kingdom of purple. Arithmetic
Belongs to the child from the fives that make the clock.
The stone that shattered Ruthie's window broke
The sun and numbers. Progression lost the garden
Where I remember
Arithmetic as cold and hard as the sun.

Yeats, Schwartz, Crane, Thomas, Auden. My eclectic education continued, although I had not yet learned the most important thing: American poets never sport a middle initial.

Working Journal

August

Chemopoetics. The subject must begin with the grape, unless rhapsodes used other drugs. Chinese poets praise drunkenness; Horace writes hymns to wine. The grape is Dionysiac by convention, and I doubt that myths arose without an historical provenance. When do other drugs come in? Romantic opium and laudanum: De Quincy, Coleridge with his self-medication, Baudelaire and the French. Now the tricyclics, Thorazine, MAO inhibitors, Lithium, Prozac . . .

Certainly in the sixties some poetry—not to mention endless prose—owed its manic rush to the laboratories of speed. Once Ted Berrigan stayed in my house for a while. All my pills disappeared: spansules supposedly for diet, pale orange Dexadrines that helped with hangovers. Ted apologized, faintly, excusing himself on account of the poems that zapped from these bottles. Some of his best things were those Ann Arbor elegies.

Reading late Auden, I note that some of the poetry—and some essays in *The Dyer's Hand*—run on with a glib chattiness that reminds me of speed, speed greater than coffee's—which as it happens is my current drug of choice: black coffee and 5 A.M.

Number 2. See "Working Journal" in *Poetry and Ambition*. These paragraphs mostly appeared in *Seneca* in 1992. Parts began in other circumstances or magazines, relocated here.

September
Every poem suggests an *ars poetica*.
In the 1960s I wrote something called "The Poem," then in the 1980s "This Poem"; they could not be more different. In between, I wrote "Ox-Cart Man" in which (as I worked on it) I had no notion that I addressed the poet's purpose or task. I wrote an *ars poetica* anyhow. The ox-cart man's endless labor makes a cycle like a perennial plant's; writing this poem, I exulted in my ox-cart man's annual rite of accumulation and dispersal. Not until I finished it, published it aloud and in print, did I become aware of a response that astonished me: Some people found it depressing: *all that work, and then he has to start over again.* (A faculty member, after a reading, said that it was like teaching freshman composition; you finish dragging through one term and then you have to start another.) Later, a friend compared the ox-cart man's story to a poet making a poem—and when I heard the suggestion, it rang true. For decades I have claimed that you must bring everything to a poem that you can possibly bring: Never hold anything back; spend everything at once— or you will never write a poem. Only when you empty the well does the water return to the well.

Flaubert said, "The idea springs from the form," which I prefer to "form is only the extension of content." The crafty Creeley said it but idiots quote it to justify *Anything Goes.* The idea springs from the form because form *denies* ideas. Snodgrass said: By attending to form we occupy the surfaces of our minds, so that forbidden content may enter the poem covertly, with our attention elsewhere.
     The Brothers Goncourt are critical. They complain that Flaubert went on "expounding with childish gravity and ridiculous solemnity ways of writing and rules for producing good prose. He attached so much importance to the clothing of an idea, to its color and material, that the idea became nothing but a peg on which to hang sound and light."

Flaubert quoted Buffon saying, "The manner in which a truth is enunciated is more useful to humanity than the truth itself." Maybe: *The manner is the truth.*

Victor Hugo carried a notebook in his pocket, not to write down what other people said, but to write down what *he* said. As he talked, if he said anything that interested him he took out his notebook.

Pound declared that sperm was a cerebral fluid. Did he find this scientific fact in Remy de Gourmont? Maybe in Balzac. The Goncourts claim that Balzac believed that "Sperms were an emission of cerebral matter and as it were a waste of creative power: and after one unfortunate incident, in the course of which he had forgotten his theories, he arrived at Latouche's exclaiming: 'I lost a book this morning.' "

It was lucky for me that I avoided Whitman when young. When I was fourteen he seemed old-fashioned and when I was twenty he seemed sloppy. My bad taste saved me Whitman for my thirties when I came to the end of several roads, private and literary. Then I found the poet of many connections and of public inwardness, who helped me out of personal and poetic cul-de-sacs. Maybe "Song of Myself" in its variety did the most; but also the original of "The Sleepers," which I found in Malcolm Cowley's edition of the 1855 *Leaves,* astonished and energized me; the tiny "A Farm Picture"; and most poignantly "Out of the Cradle." This last poem is the model of rolling speech-as-song, relentlessly pushing forward to uncover and embody connections from the present of the poet to the archaeology or provenance of original feeling, layers and strata revealed by imagination and shaped by accrual. Whitman became my companion as I lost and found myself. Others helped

me find him—Lawrence, Roethke, Ginsberg, and Kinnell—
for whom Whitman's cadences filled the sails of poetry.

Bulletin from The War between the Poets and the Philoso-
phers: David Antin: "if robert lowell is a poet i don't want to
be a poet   if robert frost was a poet i don't want to be a
poet   if socrates was a poet i'll consider it"

There's a kind of poet (Sylvia Townsend Warner, Philip
Whalen, Ted Berrigan) that one reads, not for words or
phrases, or even single poems, but to make an acquaintance or
to hear a pleasing voice. Frank O'Hara and James Schuyler also.
We become fond of the ambience, the sense of tone, the charac-
teristic *turns*. When I admire Thomas Hardy or Ezra Pound or
John Dryden, I try convincing you by saying a phrase, a line, a
quatrain. I look you in the eye and say, "Listen to this!" I can't do
this with Berrigan; you have to steep yourself in O'Hara like tea.

November
Literature is less subject to geography than theater and music,
which require cities; less than painting or sculpture, which
require expensive transport in the service of publication. Nov-
elists and poets do not need centers of population to provide
an audience, only—most of us—to supply the gregarious ri-
valry of youth by means of café or workshop. Poets need only
readers but for readers they need publishers; American writ-
ers have tended to congregate where the publishers are: Mr.
Howells from Ohio and Mr. Clemens from Missouri needed
Hartford and Boston, New York and Kittery. By 1990, as the
theater has marvelously spread west and north and south, so
publishers and poets are more happily eccentric (geographi-
cally speaking) than they used to be.

Forty years ago the American and the English read each other. For a decade or so, the English told the Americans that American poets were much better than English ones; Americans were happy to agree. Now each country's poetic culture revels in an ignorant contempt for the other, which is stupid: We are both provinces, and each province calls itself the universe. If we are different enough (and I think we are) we can learn by attending to each other.

Another matter: It used to be that poetry in England appeared under a Faber imprint, with exceptions allowed for Oxford, Deutsch, and Secker. It should be noted now that the publication of poetry in England, as in the United States, has strayed from its metropolitan center into a lively diffusion. Bloodaxe and Carcanet, to name only two, show more vitality now than the London firms—the way Graywolf and Copper Canyon are superior to New York.

When Pound translated *Cathay,* maybe French free verse showed him a way, but I'm not sure there's enough *tranquillity* in the French poems to reveal them as sources. However it came about, Pound invented a music of flatness that we have developed ever since. William Carlos Williams's strong ear for the American idiom joined and extended this music; but WCW used more enjambment and in his best work a Keatsian abundant sweetness of assonance. Rexroth developed Pound's plainness, with his own free-flowing ear for enjambment and a branching syntax. This style has become a distinguished available American mode or tone—almost a prosody.

December
Heraclitus: "Opposition unites." "Men do not understand how that which draws apart agrees with itself; harmony lies in the bending back, as for instance of the bow and of the lyre."

Heraclitus again: "One day is equal to every other." Cf. Janice Joplin: "It's always the same fucking day."

Sydney Lanier on Walt Whitman: "As near as I can make it out, Whitman's argument seems to be that because a prairie is wide therefore debauchery is admirable, and because the Mississippi is long therefore every American is God."

Trying to write a note about Fred Morgan:

The best quarterlies mostly represent one generation, one assemblage of talents and passions. When time and its losses dissipate this assemblage, the magazine dies—whether it continues to publish or not. As editor over decades, Fred Morgan has retained the *Hudson*'s standards while continuously renewing the magazine; again and again, he has discovered or recruited new writers. He has encouraged, sponsored, and commissioned work by generations, enlisting new and different names, largely (and only) consistent in quality. More than any other editor of our era, he has developed authors and critics by scouting, by praise, and by exacting revision. Discontent to represent one moment, his *Hudson* has modified or created a long series of moments.

January

When you hear poets read their poems loud, you needn't translate these sounds into the visual shape of the poem on the page; imagination of visual shape is not part of listening, and it even distracts us—as when people try to follow a reading with an open book. On the other hand, when we read poetry in solitude and silence, the visual shape on the page helps us hear the poem. Or it should. Sometimes the shape has another separate function as decorative space—like lozenge-poems, or Herbert with his angel wings; these artifices give visual pleasure as well as being semantic—

but when contemporary poets drop and isolate a word—spacing it below a previous line, detaching it in a meadow of white—if our inward-voices do not learn to pick up this word and *hold* it, we make no connection between the visual and the audible. It should go without saying: when in silence and solitude we read poetry, if our throat does not become weary, either we read bad poetry or we read good poetry badly.

When Robert Creeley wrote "Poor. Old. Tired. Horse." he wrote something composite, amusing in its violation of propriety—and *also* something that we can imitate with our voice. We will pronounce it the way we would pronounce "poor   old   tired horse," but it is more pointed to look at, and this pointedness is expressive . . .

February
"And what advice do you offer young poets, Grandfather?"

"Oh, the usual: Revise! Work! Revise! Put it away. Find it again (by chance of course) and if you can bear to read it, change it some more." As we become older and poetry becomes harder to write, we shout the old answers louder. "Don't let anything out of the house until you've written it two hundred times!" We cite Horace's ten-year moratorium (don't make it public for a decade)—halved by Pope—and end by begging for two years? . . . one year? . . . six months?

Nothing (among these non-negotiable demands) concerns the spirit of the poem, and nothing specifies the life that the poet lives. Doubtless we cherish *most* the poem's spirit; this is what we warm ourselves against, what comforts us; and doubtless the life lived is what creates or energizes the poem's spirit.

This contradiction makes no contradiction. Spirit cannot be demanded any more than it can be labeled. We cannot know it except by incarnation of comma and line-break, on account of which we may demand the scrutiny of alteration. Spirit is nameless and walks only by inhabiting word-flesh. As for the life, what job description, what reminiscence, or what thousand-page biography provides more than a stick figure? Only the poem tells the tale—not the *Who's Who* talk of "insurance executive" or "gunrunner" or "Trappist."

Therefore we slide toward the grave urging, "Revise!"

Viva control, viva expression; viva *language*. If young poets wish to become old poets they should (besides remaining alive) revise by scrutiny, patience, and stubbornness.

And when they do, they must keep an ear cocked for yet another enemy. Sometimes when we tap at a block of language for seven years and four hundred drafts, we may find ourselves changing words (punctuation, syntax, line-breaks) because we are bored with counting the same facets every day. This enemy is frivolous revision, perverse change for variety's sake: looking for trouble; *genus irritabile vatum*. In concentrating on language, fiddling with it, detaching the real from the obvious, turning words on themselves, disrupting, uprooting, maybe a skeptical critic and an over-scrupulous poet burn in the same circle.

Probably. And what is the cure? For the poet: putting the poem away, turning to other things, to cold showers or hot beds or baseball; returning to the naive view, when an apple may resemble an apple.

Death to the Death of Poetry

Some days, when you read the newspaper, it seems clear that the United States is a country devoted to poetry. You can delude yourself reading the sports pages. After finding two references to "poetry in motion," apropos of figure skating and the Kentucky Derby, you read that a shortstop is the poet of his position and that sailboats raced under blue skies that were sheer poetry. On the funny pages, Zippy praises Zerbina's outfit: "You're a poem in polyester." A funeral director, in an advertisement, muses on the necessity for poetry in our daily lives. It's hard to figure out just what he's talking about, but it becomes clear that this *poetry* has nothing to do with *poems*. It sounds more like taking naps.

Poetry, then, appears to be: 1. a vacuous synonym for excellence or unconsciousness. What else is common to the public perception of poetry?

2. It is universally agreed that no one reads it.

3. It is universally agreed that the nonreading of poetry is (a) contemporary and (b) progressive. From (a) it follows that sometime back (a wandering date, like "olden times" for a six-year-old) our ancestors read poems, and poets were rich and famous. From (b) it follows that every year fewer people read poems (or buy books or go to poetry readings) than the year before.

Other pieces of common knowledge:

4. Only poets read poetry.

This essay comes from *Harper's* magazine, 1989. Much of it appears in the Introduction to *Best American Poetry 1989.*

5. Poets themselves are to blame because "poetry has lost its audience."

6. Everybody today knows that poetry is "useless and completely out of date"—as Flaubert put it in *Bouvard and Pécuchet* a century ago.

For expansion on and repetition of these well-known facts, look in volumes of *Time* magazine, in Edmund Wilson's "Is Verse a Dying Technique?," in current newspapers everywhere, in interviews with publishers, in book reviews by poets, and in the August 1988 issue of *Commentary*, where the essayist Joseph Epstein assembled every cliché about poetry, common for two centuries, under the title "Who Killed Poetry?"

Time, which reported *The Waste Land* as a hoax in 1922, canonized T. S. Eliot in a 1950 cover story. Certainly *Time*'s writers and editors altered over thirty years, but they also stayed the same: always the Giants grow old and die, leaving the Pygmies behind. After the age of Eliot, Frost, Stevens, Moore, and Williams, the wee survivors were Lowell, Berryman, Jarrell, and Bishop. When the survivors died, younger elegiac journalists revealed that the dead Pygmies had been Giants all along—and *now* the young poets were dwarfs. Doubtless obituaries lauding Allen Ginsberg are already written; does anyone remember *Life* on the Beat Generation, thirty years ago?

"Is Verse a Dying Technique?" Edmund Wilson answered yes in 1928. It is not one of the maestro's better essays. Wilson's long view makes the point that doctors and physicists no longer use poetry when they write about medicine and the universe. Yes, Lucretius is dead. And yes, Coleridge had a notion of poetry rather different from Horace's. But Wilson also announced in 1928 that poetry had collapsed because "since the Sandburg-Pound generation, a new development in verse has taken place. The sharpness and the energy disappear; the beat gives way to a demoralized weariness." (He speaks, of course, in the heyday of Moore and Williams, Frost, H.D., Stevens, and Eliot; reprinting the essay in 1948, he added a paragraph nervously acknowledging Auden, whom he had put down twenty years before.) He goes on, amazingly, to explain the problem's source: "The trouble is that no verse technique is more obsolete today than blank verse. The old iambic pentameters have no longer any relation whatever to the tempo and language of our lives. Yeats was the last who could write them."

But Yeats wrote little blank verse of interest, bar "The Second Coming." As it happens, two Americans of Wilson's time wrote superb blank verse. (Really I should say three, because E. A. Robinson flourished in 1928. But his annual blank verse narratives were not so brilliant as his earlier work; and of course he antedated "the Sandburg-Pound generation.") Robert Frost, starting from Wordsworth, made an idiomatic American blank verse, especially in his dramatic monologues, which is possibly the best modern example of that metric; and Wallace Stevens, starting from Tennyson, made blank verse as gorgeous as "Tithonus." Read Frost's "Home Burial" and Stevens's "Sunday Morning" and then tell me that blank verse was obsolete in 1928.

Poetry was never Wilson's strong suit. It is worthwhile to remember that Wilson found Edna St. Vincent Millay the great poet of her age—better than Robert Frost, Marianne Moore, T. S. Eliot, Ezra Pound, Wallace Stevens, and William Carlos Williams. In a late self-interview by Wilson in the *New Yorker,* he revealed that among contemporary poets only Robert Lowell was worth reading. It saves a lot of time, not needing to check out Elizabeth Bishop, John Ashbery, Galway Kinnell, Louis Simpson, Adrienne Rich, Sylvia Plath, Robert Bly, John Berryman . . .

Sixty years after Edmund Wilson told us that verse was dying, Joseph Epstein in *Commentary* revealed that it was murdered. Of course, Epstein's golden age—Stevens, Frost, Williams—is Wilson's era of "demoralized weariness." Everything changes and everything stays the same. Poetry was always in good shape twenty or thirty years ago; *now* it has always gone to hell. I have heard this lamentation for forty years, not only from distinguished critics and essayists but from professors and journalists who enjoy viewing our culture with alarm.

Repetition of a formula, under changed circumstances and with different particulars, does not make formulaic complaint invalid; but surely it suggests that the formula represents something besides what it repeatedly affirms.

In asking "Who Killed Poetry?" Joseph Epstein begins by insisting that he does *not* dislike it. "I was taught that poetry was itself an exalted thing." He admits his "quasi-religious language" and asserts that "it was during the 1950s that poetry last had this religious aura." Did Epstein go to school "during the 1950s"? If he attended poetry readings in 1989 with unblinkered eyes, he would watch twenty-year-olds undergoing quasi-religious emotions—one of whom, almost certainly, will write an essay in the 2020s telling the world that poetry is moldering in its grave.

Worship is not love. People who at the age of fifty deplore the death of poetry are the same people who in their twenties were "taught to exalt it." The middle-aged poetry detractor is the student who hyperventilated at poetry readings thirty years earlier—during Wilson's "Pound-Sandburg era" or Epstein's aura-era of "T. S. Eliot and Wallace Stevens, Robert Frost and William Carlos Williams." After college many English majors stop reading contemporary poetry. Why not? They become involved in journalism or scholarship, essay writing or editing, brokerage or social work; they backslide from the undergraduate Church of Poetry. Years later, glancing belatedly at the poetic scene, they tell us that poetry is dead. They left poetry; therefore they blame poetry for leaving them. Really, they lament their own aging. Don't we all? But some of us do not blame the current poets.

Epstein localizes his attack on two poets, unnamed but ethnically specified: "One of the two was a Hawaiian of Japanese ancestry, the other was middle-class Jewish." (They were Garrett Hongo and Edward Hirsch, who testified on behalf of American poetry to the National Council of the Arts, where Joseph Epstein as a Councillor regularly assured his colleagues that contemporary American writing was dreck.) Epstein speaks disparagingly of these "Japanese" and "Jewish" poets, in his ironic mosquito whine, and calls their poems "heavily preening, and not distinguished enough in language or subtlety of thought to be memorable."

Such disparagement is pure blurbtalk. He does not quote a line by either poet he dismisses. As with the aging Edmund Wilson, Epstein saves time by ignoring particulars of the art he disparages.

Dubious elegies on the death of poetry shouldn't need answers. A frequently reported lie, however, can turn into fact. In his essay, Joseph Epstein tells us that "last year the *Los Angeles Times* announced it would no longer review books of poems." In the *Washington Post,* Jonathan Yardley referred to the same event, which never happened, and applauded what never happened except in his own negligent error.

The editor of the *Los Angeles Times Book Review* announced that his paper would review *fewer* books; instead, the *Review* would print a whole poem in a box every week, with a note on the poet. In the years since instituting this policy, *LATBR* has continued to review poetry—more than the *New York Times Book Review* has done—and in addition has printed an ongoing anthology of contemporary American verse. The *Los Angeles Times* probably pays more attention to poetry than any other newspaper in the country.

Yet when the *LAT* announced its new policy, poets picketed the paper. Poets love to parade as victims; we love the romance of alienation and insult.

More than a thousand poetry books appear in this country each year. More people write poetry in this country—publish it, hear it, and presumably read it—than ever before. Let us quickly and loudly proclaim that no poet sells like Stephen King, that poetry is not as popular as professional wrestling, and that fewer people attend poetry readings in the United States than in Russia. Snore, snore. More people read poetry now in the United States than ever did before.

When I was in school in the 1940s, there were few poetry readings; only Frost did many. If we consult biographies of Stevens and Williams, we understand that for them a poetry reading was an unusual event. In these decades, the magazine

Poetry printed on its back cover Walt Whitman's claim that "to have great poets there must be great audiences too" but it seemed an idle notion at the time. Then readings picked up in the late 1950s, avalanched in the 1960s, and continue unabated in the 1990s. Readings sell books. When trade publishers in 1950 issued a third book by a prominent poet, they printed hardbound copies, possibly a thousand. If the edition sold out in three or four years, everybody was happy. The same trade publisher in 1989 would likely print the same poet in an edition of five thousand, hard and soft—and the book would stand a good chance of being reprinted, at least in paper. Recently, a dozen or more American poets have sold at least some of their books by the tens of thousands: Adrienne Rich, Robert Bly, Allen Ginsberg, John Ashbery, Galway Kinnell, Robert Creeley, Gary Snyder, Denise Levertov, Carolyn Forché; doubtless others. Last I knew, Galway Kinnell approached fifty thousand—over the years—with *Book of Nightmares*.

It is not only the sales of books that one can adduce to support the notion that poetry's audience has grown tenfold in the last thirty years. If poetry readings provide the largest new audience, there are also more poetry magazines, and those magazines sell more copies. In 1955 no one would have believed you if you had suggested that two or three decades hence the United States would support a bimonthly poetry tabloid with a circulation of twenty thousand available on newsstands coast to coast. Everybody complains about the *American Poetry Review;* nobody acknowledges how remarkable it is that it exists.

A few years back, a journal of the publishing industry printed a list of all-time trade paperback best-sellers, beginning with *The Joy of Sex,* which sold millions, on down to books that had sold two hundred fifty thousand. It happened that I read the chart shortly after learning that Lawrence Ferlinghetti's *Coney Island of the Mind,* a trade paperback, had sold more than a million copies. Because the book was poetry, the journal understood that its sales did not count.

When I make these points, I encounter fierce resistance. No one wants to believe me. If ever I convince people that these numbers are correct, they come up with excuses: Bly sells because he's a showman; Ginsberg is notorious; Rich sells because of feminist politics. People come up with excuses for these numbers because the notion of poetry's disfavor is important—to poetry's detractors and to its supporters. Why does almost everyone connected with poetry claim that poetry's audience has diminished? Doubtless the pursuit of failure and humiliation is part of it. There is also a source that is lovable if unobservant: Some of us love poetry so dearly that its absence from *everybody's* life seems an outrage. Our parents don't read James Merrill! Therefore, exaggerating out of foiled passion, we claim that "nobody reads poetry."

When I contradict such notions, at first I insist merely on numbers. If everybody artistic loathes statistics, everybody artistic still tells us that "nobody reads poetry," which is a numerical notion—and untrue. Of course, the numbers I recite have nothing whatsoever to do with the quality or spirit of the poetry sold or read aloud. I include no Rod McKuen in my figures; I include only poetry that intends artistic excellence. My numbers counter only numbers—and not assertions of value and its lack.

But I need as well, and separately, to insist: I believe in the quality of the best contemporary poetry; I believe that the best American poetry of our day makes a considerable literature. *American Poetry after Lowell*—an anthology of four hundred pages limited, say, to women and men born from the 1920s through the 1940s—would collect a large body of diverse, intelligent, beautiful, moving work that should endure. Mind you, it would limit itself to one-hundredth of one percent of the poems published. If you write about Poetry Now, you must acknowledge that *most* poetry is terrible—that *most* poetry of *any* moment is terrible. When, at any historical moment, you write an article claiming that poetry is now in terrible shape, you are *always* right. Therefore, you are *always* fatuous.

Our trouble is not with poetry but with the public perception of poetry. Although we have more poetry today, we have less poetry reviewing in national journals. Both *Harper's* magazine and the *Atlantic* have abandoned quarterly surveys of poetry. The *New York Times Book Review* never showed much interest, but as poetry has increased in popularity, the *Times* has diminished its attention. The *New York Review of Books*, always more political than poetical, gives poetry less space every year. The greatest falling-off is at the *New Yorker*. The *New Yorker* once regularly published Louise Bogan's essays on "Verse." Lately, when the magazine touches on poetry, Helen Vendler is more inclined to write about a translation or about a poet safely dead. In the past, men and women like Conrad Aiken, Malcolm Cowley, and Louise Bogan practiced literary journalism to make a living. Their successors now meet classes MWF. People with tenure don't need to write book reviews.

Their absence is poetry's loss, and the poetry reader's—for we need a cadre of reviewers to sift through the great volume of material. The weight of numbers discourages readers from trying to keep up. More poetry than ever: How do we discriminate? How do we find or identify beautiful new work? When there are sufficient reviewers, who occupy continual soapboxes and promote developing standards, they provide sensors to report from the confusing plentitude of the field.

Beside the weight of numbers, another perennial source of confusion is partisanship. When I was in my twenties and writing iambic stanzas, Allen Ginsberg's *Howl* was a living reproach. For a while I denigrated Allen: "If he's right, I must be wrong." Such an either/or is silly and commonplace: restrictions are impoverishments. In the 1920s one was not allowed to admire both T. S. Eliot and Thomas Hardy; it was difficult for intellectuals who admired Wallace Stevens and his bric-a-brac to find houseroom for Robert Frost and his subjects. Looking back at the long heyday of modern poetry, removed by time from partisanship, we can admire the era's virtuosity, the *various* excellences of these disparate characters born in the 1870s and 1880s, who knew each other and wrote as if they didn't. What foursome could be more dissimilar than Moore, Williams, Stevens, and Frost? Maybe the answer is: some foursome right now.

✤There are a thousand ways to love a poem. The best poets make up new ways, and the new ways mostly take getting used to. The poetry reading helps toward understanding (which explains how poetry thrives without book reviewing) because the poet's voice and gesture provide entrance to the poetry: a way in, a hand at the elbow. The poetry reading helps—but as a substitute for reviewing it is inefficient. And sometimes it is hard to know whether we cherish the poem or its performance.

At least there are many poets, many readings—and there *is* an audience. For someone like me, born in the 1920s, which produced great poetry and neglected to read it—Knopf remaindered Wallace Stevens—our poetic moment is inspiriting. As I grew up, from the 1930s to the 1950s, poets seldom read aloud and felt lucky to sell a thousand copies. In the 1990s the American climate for poetry is infinitely more generous. In the mail, in the rows of listeners, even in the store down the road, I find generous response. I find it in magazines and in rows of listeners in Pocatello and Akron, in Florence, South Carolina, and in Quartz Mountain, Oklahoma. I find it in books published and in extraordinary sales for many books.

While most readers and poets agree that "nobody reads poetry"— and we warm ourselves by the gregarious fires of our solitary art—maybe a multitude of nobodies assembles the great audience Whitman looked for.

Thom Gunn Resisting

Thom Gunn has lived in San Francisco for thirty years, writing powerful intelligent poems out of friendship and solitude. He was born in England fifty-nine years ago. His mother, he tells us, read Gibbon while he was in the womb; his father excelled as a journalist, the Beaverbrook sort, and eventually became editor of the tabloid *Daily Sketch*. But his parents were divorced when he was eight and his mother died when he was fifteen; Gunn's intransigent independence, which characterizes the man and the work, made virtue out of necessity.

After finishing secondary school in London, Gunn served two years in the British Army before he went up to Trinity College, most artistic or intellectual of Cambridge institutions. Before he was graduated in 1953, he was known as a poet.

Thom Gunn, therefore, is an English poet: except that he isn't. Nor is he American. The point is not legalities of citizenship (Gunn remains a resident alien, fitting a poet both domestic and estranged) but that he may not be labeled by nationality or anything else: His identity is his resistance to the limitations of identity. He belongs to uncertainty, movement, exploration, and ongoingness. His early motorcycle poem, "On the Move," says all that Gunn cares to say about permanent addresses when it famously ends: "One is always nearer by not keeping still." Here is the man without conventional supports, who refuses title and easychair, political party and national identity. For Thom Gunn, affiliation is a lie; only change endures.

His poetry embodies such notions; my paraphrase blurs

This essay was written for the *Los Angeles Times Book Review* when Thom Gunn won its Robert Kirsch Award in 1988.

them into prose. If he is a poet of thought, his ideas express themselves in poetry's ethic of condensation and corrosive self-cancellation: Gunn's ideas occupy poetry not philosophy. The philosopher who makes apothegms like Nietzsche (or like Heraclitus in his fragments) may approach this embodiment of thought; but poetry embodies best. The lines of Gunn's verse, with their pauses and contradictions, word crossing out word, express and withhold in accurate measure. Gunn ends an early poem, "In Santa Maria del Populo," by describing Caravaggio's Saint Paul: "Resisting, by embracing, nothingness." Poetry exists in order to express such a wholeness.

Thom Gunn is least known among the best living poets. In England he is suspect because he defected to the United States; in America he is suspect as an Englishman. Ridiculously, each country refuses to read the other's poets—and Gunn's readership suffers twice because he is citizen of both countries and of neither. In the United States, where poets perform on platforms, he has not ingratiated himself on the poetry-reading circuit. He teaches as little as he may—one term a year at Berkeley provides him support—and keeps house in San Francisco.

If he belongs to a nation it is San Francisco; or perhaps homosexuality is a country—but I do not find him pledging allegiance to anything except his own alert, unforgiving, skeptical independence. I think of Stephen Dedalus telling Cranly about the voices that ask you to heed them: family, friends, country, church. Thom Gunn's poetic voice sings out of his chosen isolation, a man without a country, in exploration of the value and power of the solitude of spirit which all men share and few admit. Gunn wears the badge *noli me tangere* in a house of friends.

When he was still young he wrote with astonishing skill. I remember the general flabbergast when Thom Gunn's first poems went public. In 1952 when his poetry came roaring out of Cambridge, I was at Oxford among the young Shelleys, an alien (older, slightly bewildered) poetic technician from the United States. In Oxford writing poetry was a social accomplishment; it got you invited to parties; it got you mentioned in *Isis* gossip columns. If there *were* people who took poetry seriously, like Christopher Middleton, they mostly concealed themselves. The extraordinary Geoffrey Hill, who was twenty years old, mumbled in hiding the great epithets of "Genesis." Most Oxford poets believed in sincerity, amateurishness, villanelles, adjectives, love, and good manners. Cambridge, they thought, stalled in a critical doldrum, leaving poetry to the sweet singers of Oxford. Imagine the consternation when Thom Gunn's "The Secret Sharer" broadcast its firm structures on the BBC in the autumn of 1952, and a little later, "Incident on a Journey." Both poems appeared on John Lehmann's *New Soundings* Third Programme magazine. "Incident on a Journey" varied a refrain that claimed "I regret nothing," which was disturbing at Oxford, where the poets regretted practically everything.

Oxford recoiled before stanzas militant, intransigent, tough, brainy, swashbuckling, and violent. It's always useful, looking at a mature poet, to remember what he looked like from the other side. It may surprise readers in 1988 that in the 1950s Gunn shocked the English public because of his violence. His apparent violence has been overshadowed by the language, red in tooth and claw, of Ted Hughes who came later out of Cambridge—more muscular, less philosophical. The two poets do not resemble each other. Hughes insinuates himself into the skin of a crow or a pike, man turning animal in flight from reason, while Gunn embraces action for reasons; by his metaphors, analogies, agonies, contradictions, and rhythms he argues a way to live, or a way to understand living. Gunn seemed violent in 1953 only as he burst upon British gentility. His pentameters trumpeting of wars, wounds, and journeys interrupted the tea party.

What an interruption it was. Not only Oxford noticed. In England of the 1950s ambitious undergraduates from Oxbridge expected to shift from the university to London—politicians from the Oxford Union to Parliament, actors from OUDs to the Old Vic—with a quick depression of the clutch. Hadn't Kenneth Tynan done it? Strangely enough, London seemed to agree with Oxbridge. When John Lehmann started a new radio magazine, he recruited his innovations among Oxbridge undergraduates. Can you imagine an American editor going to Harvard and Yale, to Stanford and Berkeley undergraduates in quest of discovery? Sandbagged by Thom Gunn, Oxford's poets *did* something about it. If you feel under attack in England, you invite your enemy to your club. Gunn came to Oxford for a weekend. At a party the Oxford poets met this modest terror and found him agreeable; maybe the universe could accommodate one more poet. A few weeks later in Cambridge Gunn walked me around to meet his friends.

The following year I found myself in California, working with Yvor Winters at Stanford on a writing fellowship, writing letters from Menlo Park to my English poet-friends. I knew that Gunn was desperate to find a way to the United States. I suggested that he apply for the same fellowship the next year; he did, Winters liked his work—and Gunn came to California.

Thom Gunn worked with Winters for a year, left for a year, and came back to work with him again. The relationship proved useful. Gunn admired Winters and learned from him. For many students, it was difficult to learn from Winters without dwindling into a junior lookalike. Like Leavis in England— whose lectures Gunn attended—Yvor Winters created sons not brothers; many Wintersians proved incapable of growing up. Gunn's intransigency protected him, although he loved the man; Gunn has written the best essay on Winters. He went his own way, making mistakes that Winters would have protected him from, but making as well discoveries or innovations that Winters would have protected him from.

While he was at Stanford Gunn began to experiment—the formally conservative Winters had experimented as a young man—especially with syllabics, in which he would do some of his best work. In iambic he has kept a sure, strong marching ear—but some poems need not march, or if they march they tell lies. With "My Sad Captains" and other poems, Gunn has explored beautifully in syllabic lines, and he has learned to improvise in free verse, studying the practice of American contemporaries. (His essay on Robert Creeley is the best we have on Creeley; Gunn writes few essays but they stay written.) By now, Thom Gunn has worked at his craft until he can do what he pleases; and in the availability of his styles, he strides the Atlantic. The swashbuckling young Gunn, Ancient Pistol himself on occasion, has disappeared, replaced by a tone deceptively gentle—deceptive only because the understanding (which the tone enforces) remains courageous, bleak, and uncompromising. The free verse "Elegy," which begins *The Passages of Joy*, ends by making an American sound:

> An odd comfort
> that the way we are always
> most in agreement
> is in playing the same game
> where everyone always gets lost

Yet it is worth notice: In the rhythm of free verse Gunn still lets us understand that resisting is embracing.

Back to Berryman

When I was at Oxford I knew a Rhodes Scholar, graduated from Princeton, who had studied with John Berryman. At the time, readers of poetry knew only the John Berryman of *The Dispossessed*. Everything else lay ahead: *Homage to Mistress Bradstreet, The Dream Songs,* prizes, love, and fame—or maybe only what passes, in America, for the last infirmity of noble minds: *Life*'s portrait of the wild drunken poet. The Rhodes Scholar told me in 1952 that Berryman had given up poetry and would devote himself to becoming a Shakespearean scholar. "*Anything,*" the young Princetonian told me, "*anything* rather than be a minor poet."

When *Homage* came out in *Partisan Review,* two years later, it was not clear that Berryman had risen to the heights I was told he disdained. After all, Gray is a minor poet, Cowper, Ralegh, Vaughan, Traherne, Collins, Arnold, even Hopkins perhaps—writers whom Eliot might have had in mind when he confided that his own status as a minor poet was secure: To be a minor poet, in the tradition of English and American literature, is a considerable achievement.

For readers who weigh poets in th'eternal scales, Berryman remains a problem. Rereading all the poems after I suffered through Paul Mariani's biography, from time to time I felt disgust with the work—which is perhaps better than feeling nothing, but not much better. Sometimes Berryman sought excellence by looking in the mirror and writing slack prosaic lines that expressed self-absorption:

A review of *Berryman's Understanding,* edited by Harry Thomas, and *Dream Song* by Paul Mariani.

> I must further explain: I needed a B,
> I didn't need an A, as in my other six courses,
>
> but the extra credits accruing from those A's
> would fail to accrue if I'd any mark under B.
> The bastard knew this,
> as indeed my predicament was well known

Or he would try redeeming banality through affectation:

> At Harvard & Yale must Pussy-cat be heard
> in the dead of winter when we must be sad
> and feel by the weather had.

But, each time before I closed the book, I read language that snatched me back: a newly found, rarely excellent late dream song perhaps, or a devotional poem of his twilight conversion.

Examples later. I'm not alone in my confusion: Berryman remains a problem for many critics in *Berryman's Understanding*, a collection of essays well edited by Harry Thomas. When Philip Toynbee reviews *77 Dream Songs*, he introduces some stanzas by remarking shrewdly, "Here are a few verses which may help to give a flavor of Berryman's latest method"—and then reveals that two of them are his own pastiche. (I spotted one and missed the other, which sounds like pretty *good* Berryman.) By and large the English write about Berryman better than the Americans do. Berryman brought home from his time at Cambridge a short-lived English accent and an enduring if grudging Anglophilia; the English have returned the compliment by the seriousness of their critical attention. Among Americans in *Berryman's Understanding*, Robert Lowell contributes a touching, exquisite memoir; John Frederick Nims writes a strong skeptical essay; but the best essays here belong to Douglas Dunn, Denis Donaghue, and John Bayley. Two interviews with the poet prove useful or entertaining. In the Peter Stitt interview, five footnotes provide testimony to poetic bipolarity. Berryman was high and sober for the interview, befuddled with megalomania, speaking of "People like Jefferson, Poe, and me." Later, with the alternations of blood chemistry, he footnoted these remarks: "Delusion."

The one time I met him he was sober and high, smoking innumerable cigarettes and drinking cup after cup of black coffee. It was 1968, I think, and I read my poems in Minneapolis; a messenger brought me Berryman's invitation. (Some years before, Faber had commissioned me to edit a new version of Michael Roberts's *Faber Book of Modern Verse,* and I had happily included several of the *77 Dream Songs* as well as a patch from *Homage.* Berryman had grown up on Roberts's *Faber Book,* and it delighted him to enter its reedited pages.) That afternoon, Berryman was cordial, intelligent, solemn, and overconfident; he told me that he had just completed three hundred and eight new dream songs. My heart sank. (We were about to witness Robert Lowell's deterioration through manic overproduction, but Berryman led the way as the rivals outswooned each other.) My heart-sinking was accurate enough, I think, for of the three hundred and eight new dream songs there are fewer than ten as good as the best twenty from the earlier book. Everyone cites 145, on his father's suicide:

Also I love him: me he's done no wrong
for going on forty years—forgiveness time—
I touch now his despair,
he felt as bad as Whitman on his tower
but he did not swim out with me or my brother
as he threatened—

a powerful swimmer, to take one of us along
as company in the defeat sublime,
freezing my helpless mother:
he only,   very early in the morning,
rose with his gun and went outdoors by my window
and did what was needed.

I cannot read that wretched mind, so strong
& so undone. I've always tried. I—I'm
trying to forgive
whose frantic passage, when he could not live
an instant longer, in the summer dawn
left Henry to live on.

There's also 168:

> and God has many other surprises, like
> when the man you fear most in the world marries your
>   mother
> and chilling other,
> men from far tribes armed in the dark, the dike-
> hole, the sudden gash of an old friend's betrayal,
> words out that leave one pale,
>
> milk & honey in the old house, mouth gone bad,
> the caress that felt for all the world like a blow,
> screams of fear eyeless, wide-eyed loss,
> hellish vaudeville turns, promises had
> & promises forgotten here below,
> the final wound of the Cross.
>
> I have a story to tell you which is the worst
> story to tell that ever once I heard.
> What thickens my tongue?
> and has me by the throat? I gasp accursed
> even for the thought of uttering that word.
> I pass to the next Song:

In some weaker examples, Berryman writes counting on the reader's knowledge of his life—Lowell also sometimes writes as if for subscribers to the *Robert Lowell Newsletter*—but the best *Dream Songs* survive on their own merits. Other than 168, the best of the later *Songs* are: 197, 266, 294, 382, and (maybe best of all) 384:

> The marker slants, flowerless, day's almost done,
> I stand above my father's grave with rage,
> often, often before
> I've made this awful pilgrimage to one
> who cannot visit me, who tore his page
> out: I come back for more,
>
> I spit upon this dreadful banker's grave
> who shot his heart out in a Florida dawn
> O ho alas alas
> When will indifference come, I moan & rave

I'd like to scrabble till I got right down
away down under the grass

and ax the casket open ha to see
just how he's taking it, which he sought so hard
we'll tear apart
the mouldering grave clothes ha & then Henry
will heft the ax once more, his final card,
and fell it on the start.

Back to the ur-subject. As we read the weak majority of these poems, we are annoyed by narcissism, complacency, and self-importance. Yet we keep on reading them. They are—as one says of journalism—*readable;* often when they fail as whole poems, they remain interesting for bits and pieces. The most debilitating quality in the *Dream Songs* is Berryman's gross alcoholic self-pity. (Self-pity is the major emotion expressed by American poets born between 1913 and 1917.) The seminal text remains Lewis Hyde's *Alcohol and Poetry: John Berryman and the Booze Talking,* in which Hyde founds the science of chemopoetics (most commentary on alcoholism and the American writer is mere anecdote) that will eventually investigate the effects of Thorazine on Lowell and Sexton, not to mention amphetamines on a host of poets from the East Village to Boulder and Bolinas. But alcohol creates the plupart of chemopoems to date—malt more than Milton—and Hyde is its first anatomist. I wish Harry Thomas had used Hyde's essay for *Berryman's Understanding.*

For a vision of Berryman's literary intelligence unencumbered by self-pity, it's useful to look at his essays. As often with a poet who puzzles us, his criticism helps us read his poetry. *The Freedom of the Poet* includes nothing better than his work on Nash, Marlow, and Shakespeare—criticism founded on scholarship—in which we find him celebrating Elizabethan syntax for its expressive distortion by rupture and eccentricity; thus we discover one source for the poet's style. Here also Berryman is eloquent on Anne Frank and brilliant in praise of Henry James's late revisions, for the New York Edition, against an unholy consensus that prefers the early versions. In these essays, Berryman's literary intelligence and learning are exemplary, deeper than Jarrell's in his own generation. Apparently these qualities accompanied him to the classroom; I gather from many poets who worked with Berryman that his passion and eloquence made him a great teacher.

Berryman's generation in retrospect is strong but perverse, finally more mannered than accomplished, more passively suffering than triumphant. These poets—Schwartz, Jarrell, Lowell, and Berryman—were single-minded in devotion to their art at the expense of everything and everybody else. *Lord Weary's Castle* (1947) comes closest to greatness; then in his late work Lowell settled for personality and manner. Berryman also discovered a manner (suitable for expressing anxiety, guilt, torment, self-pity, and self-justification) and if *The Dream Songs* include few *poems,* the manner parcels out much *poetry.* His voices told Yeats: We bring you metaphors for poetry; then they revealed the structures of history. One voice told Berryman one method: *Open the forbidden door, because without agony you lack a subject.* Berryman told an interviewer that he wanted to be *nearly* crucified. Suffering is a worthy subject, but possibly it ought not to stop with one's own.

The life, undertaken to make literature, was a mess. If we read Mariani for the plot, *Dream Song* resembles a disaster highlight film, *Great Car Wrecks of Mid-Century.* Or maybe it's a Demolition Derby, for these car wrecks are purposeful. However, it's difficult to read Mariani for the plot; his prose keeps getting in the way. Some of Mariani's efforts belong in the Wandering Sentence Hall of Fame:

> Across the Mississippi River, at the west-bank campus, near the once-notorious Five Corners section of the city whose bars Berryman often frequented and where he wrote so many of his early *Dream Songs,* is the library that houses special collections and rare books, and here is every letter Berryman ever wrote to his mother, along with Berryman's evaluations of teaching assistants and other documents, and I want to thank Austin McLean, curator, for his patience and help with this collection.

On many occasions, Professor Mariani does not quite understand ordinary English words. When he tells us that Berryman "remained magnetized and repulsed by women," we understand that although Berryman *was* repulsed from time to time, Mariani reached for the word "repelled" and never quite found it. Elsewhere he praises Berryman for "recalling the details of the film with amazing attention to detail." However, it is in onomastic invention that Mariani shines most brightly. We may be used to Ivor Winters, we may find John Silken almost commonplace, but *who* except Mariani would invent an English poet named Steven Spender? Best of all, he continually drops the name of the English critic Tony Alvarez. Even in the index, this early advocate of Berryman's verse is never addressed by his bookjacket name of A. Alvarez, but always by the familiar Tony. Alas, A. stands for Albert not Anthony and Mr. Alvarez's cronies call him Al. "Tony Alvarez" reminds me of those folks, years back, who told us stories about their pal "Bob Lowell."

John Berryman spent his life writing poems, and left behind two volumes amalgamating more than six hundred pages— including thirty *Dream Songs* worth keeping, two good early poems, an occasionally brilliant *Homage,* and six examples of late work as strong as this last section of "Eleven Addresses to the Lord":

> Germanicus leapt upon the wild lion in Smyrna,
> wishing to pass quickly from a lawless life.
> - The crowd shook the stadium.
> The proconsul marvelled.
>
> 'Eighty & six years have I been his servant,
> and he has done me no harm.
> How can I blaspheme my King who saved me?'
> Polycarp, John's pupil, facing the fire.
>
> Make too me acceptable at the end of time
> in my degree, which then Thou wilt award.
> Cancer, senility, mania,
> I pray I may be ready with my witness.

With such poems it's possible—I'm not ready to swear it—that John Berryman accomplished the prodigy of becoming a minor poet.

Interview with Liam Rector

You've written poignantly about time and generations. José Ortega y Gasset had a scheme for generation:

Ages:	1 to 15	Childhood
	15 to 30	Youth
	30 to 45	Initiation
	45 to 60	Dominance
	60 to 75	Old Age, "Outside of Life"

How have these moments moved in consort with the time of your life, your work, and the scheme of literary generations as you've experienced them?

Schemes irritate me. Maybe this scheme annoys me because I'm supposed to move "outside of life" in a few months and I'm damned if I'm ready to. Rigidities, separations get my back up. Maybe I left childhood at fourteen and remained adolescent until forty-three. I like the word "dominance"— and I suppose I felt it first about fifty, though I think I was looking for it from the age of fifteen. So I respond, not by generality on the schemer's level, but autobiographically or egotistically. Chronological skeletons—like somatic or psychological types, like classes, like historical determinism: hell, like the goddamned horoscope!—provide things to talk about, frameworks for discussion . . . But if you accept them, if you do not rebel against them, you actively desire the comfort of prison! Everything's done for you; relax: prison . . . or *tenure.*

In the essay, "Rusticus," you said you grew up in Hamden, Connecticut, a suburb of New Haven, in a "massclass" neighborhood wherein everyone more or less shared four convictions: (1) I will do better than my father and mother; (2) My children will do better than I do; (3) "Better" includes "education," and education provides the things of this world; (4) The things of this world are good. String Too Short to Be Saved *speaks powerfully for the summer life in New Hampshire you experienced as a boy, but could you say more about the culture and class in which you grew up in Hamden?* Have you done better?

In the suburban neighborhood where I grew up in Connecticut, the houses were like each other; the cars that belonged to the houses resembled each other; the fathers, working at their different jobs, had incomes roughly similar; the mothers weren't supposed to work, and their leisure or volunteer-work decorated the fathers. In school, there were rewards for conformity and punishments for difference. In the culture of the country, where I spent my summers, there was fantastic diversity—in education, aspiration, income, appearance; what you wore, what you ate, what you did for fun—from house to house along the roads and lanes. Eccentricity was a *value;* a major ethical notion was everybody's right to be different. I belonged to the Connecticut culture and longed for the other. I live in the other now—it's not greatly changed—and live by it, observe it, write about it, but of course I will never be truly *of* it. My whole life comes out of the conflict of these cultures— and my choice to love and inhabit the one rather than the other.

You went to the Phillips Exeter Academy and then to Harvard, Oxford, and Stanford. Did the students at these schools share the cultural and class background you outlined in the essay "Rusticus"? You then went on to the public, sprawling world of the University of Michigan to teach. What led you to attend these schools as a student, and what went into the decision to teach at Michigan?

The class structure in England is unlike ours, and I won't try to describe it. Sure, other students at Exeter were mostly from the same suburbs, where people try to resemble each other, but most came from more money than I did. My parents sent me there because they knew it was a good school, I don't think for social reasons at all. They weren't social people. At Exeter the best teachers all came from Harvard; the best students were going there. Quickly I knew I wanted to go there. Some Exeter kids came from money that had been around in the family longer. At Harvard I felt less of this. There was more diversity there, at least among the people I knew. Even at that time, Harvard was more high school than prep school, trying to get the best high school students from all over the country. They were a bunch of tigers locked in a small cage; I liked that. I tried for a fellowship to Oxford because it was a plum and because it sounded like fun to travel and live in another country. While I was there England was in a bad way economically. I never saw my English friends on the continent during holiday because they were only allowed to take twenty-five pounds out of the country that year. There were already lots of scholarship boys at Oxford, but I was so separate culturally—older, from another nation. Being an outsider gave me privileges which I enjoyed, privileges to be weird.

One of the reasons I went to the University of Michigan was to get away from the Harvard I liked so much. After I did the B.A., I spent only three years away at first—Oxford and Stanford—then returned for three more years in the Society of Fellows. There were pathetic sorts around the Square who would take any sort of rotten job in order not to leave Cambridge, or—perish the thought!—go to the *Middle West*. (America's geographical snobbery is repulsive.) I wanted to get away, to try another kind of institution, and Michigan made a good offer. Ironically—probably predictably!—I went to an institution that, within Michigan and nearby states, is considered rather snobbish, rather old school tie. Some students' grandparents and parents had belonged to the same fraternities and sororities—but there were also the children of lineworkers. I liked that variety, that looseness.

We both grew up spending our summers with our grandparents on farms, you in New Hampshire and I in Virginia. In String *you wrote of how this shaped your imagination and that residence where imagination and memory commingle. Living now on that same farm where you spent summers, what is your memory, your imagination of the large cities?*

I've never lived in a great city. For me, large cities are excitement, energy, vitality, almost mania. When I go to New York I never sleep. Oh, I've lived for a month or two at a time in London, Paris, Rome. Because Cambridge is virtually Boston, and I went to school there, I suppose I *did* live in a big city—but living in a college isn't the same. I contrast the country not to the city but to the suburbs; Ann Arbor is a suburb without an urb. (Technically it's a city.)

This place is no longer a farm but the rural culture remains amazingly intact, although thirty years ago I thought it was vanishing. I love the landscape more deeply all the time; I am content sitting on the porch and gazing at Kearsarge; or walking in the woods. Carol Bly speaks somewhere of writers who are "mindless nature describers." Maybe I'm a mindless nature lover, but I love also the independence and solitude of the country, which is by no means only a matter of population density. I don't suffer from the deference, mostly ironic, that hangs around writers in universities; here, I'm the "fellow over there who writes books for a living" and that's a freedom.

Your work has been haunted not only by the grandfather but the father. Did your father encourage you to become a writer?

My father was soft and volatile, a businessman who hated being a businessman and daydreamed for himself a life in the academy—probably prep school rather than college—where everybody would be *kind* to everybody else. He read books; mostly he read contemporary historical fiction like Hervey Allen and Kenneth Roberts. Politically he was conservative and not very thoughtful. He wept frequently and showed feelings which other men would hold back. He desperately wanted people to like him and many did. He was nervous, continually shaking; quick, alert, sensitive, unintellectual. When he was forty-two he hemorrhaged with a bad bleeding ulcer and remained sickly until he got lung cancer at fifty-one and died at fifty-two. As an adolescent I needed to feel superior to him; when I was about twenty-five, when my son was born, I felt reconciled. I don't think we talked about matters of great substance but we could love each other. He read my things and mostly praised them, but I don't think either of us wanted to talk about them. He tried to encourage me in one direction, constantly, by telling me that my poetry was just fine but my prose was really great. Some of this at least was his desire that I might possibly be able to make a living. When he realized that I was going into teaching, it pleased him because of his imaginary academy.

Your new book, The One Day, *is in many ways a departure from* Kicking the Leaves *and* The Happy Man, *both in its elliptical form, its being a book-length shoring of fragments, and its engagement with the very old and the very new, aside from your personal remembered past, which sets much of the tone in the two books before. How do you account for this shift? One section of* The One Day, *"Shrubs Burnt Away," was printed in* The Happy Man. *What made you decide to foreshadow the long poem by printing it there? Had you yet seen the shape that* The One Day *would assume?*

If you look at my poems from the beginning in 1955, there is lot of moving about and shifting. Surely you're right that the form of *The One Day* is modernist, with its multiple protagonist—but I guess I don't want to . . . Really, I don't want to talk about the form of it. It's new; I'm still finding out what I did.

The poem began with an onslaught of language back in 1971. Over a period of weeks I kept receiving messages; I filled page after page of notebooks. If I drove to the supermarket, I had to bring the book and pull over three or four times in a few miles to transcribe what was coming. It was inchoate, sloppy, but full of *material:* verbal, imaginative, recollected. And it was frightening. After a while the barrage ceased, but from time to time over the years more would come—with a little label on it, telling me that it belonged to this *thing*. (In my head for a long time I called it *Building the House of Dying*.) The first part was there in inchoate form, much of the first two of "Four Classic Texts," much of the "one day" theme in the third part. Every now and then, over the years, I would look at these notebooks, and feel excitement and fear. In 1980 I began to *work* on it; to try to do something with these words. First I set it out as a series of twenty-five or thirty linked free verse poems: Nothing marched. I worked on it for a year or two; I remember reading it aloud to Jane one time, and when I finished I was full of *shame*. Shame over what I revealed, shame over bad poetry; after that, I couldn't look at it for a year.

At some point early in the 1980s, Robert Mazzocco suggested casually in a letter that I ought sometime to write a book of linked poems. Thinking of this notion I developed my ten-line stanza, making some into almost discrete ten-line poems, using others as stanzas. I thought of Keats's *Ode* stanza, developed out of the sonnet and the desire to write the longer ode form. This notion helped me get to work: bricks— cement blocks?—for the house. I worked with these stanzas for a couple of years, then maybe in 1984 developed a three-part idea that *somewhat* resembles the present version, except that the middle part is totally different. I showed a draft to a few people. I remember Bly saying, with his usual diffidence, that the first part was the *best* thing I had ever done and the second part was the *worst* thing I had ever done. The second part was a problem until I worked out the notion that turned into "Four Classic Texts"; I stole "Eclogue" from Vergil, which always helps. Even after I had the Classic Texts, I thought the third part was my real problem, and sometimes doubted that I would ever finish the whole—because I wouldn't be able to make the third part.

When I put *The Happy Man* together I had "Shrubs Burnt Away" more or less finished, "Four Classic Texts" beginning, and "In the One Day" lying about in pieces. I thought it would be ten years before I would be able to finish the poem as a whole, if I ever did. I had no notion that I might finish it within a couple of years. But I think that printing "Shrubs" in *The Happy Man* allowed me to finish the whole poem. Response was encouraging . . . and some reviews helped me understand what I was doing, like David Shapiro's in *Poetry*, with his reference to Freud and the movement from hysterical misery to ordinary unhappiness!

What about your work in children's books?

I've worked on children's books for twenty-five years, starting when Andrew was a little boy, and I've written many—but only published four. The first was *Andrew the Lion Farmer*, which I may rewrite and reissue. That one came out of story-telling with Andrew when he was four years old. I made up lots of stories. Then one day he said he had a great, scary idea: He was going to go to the lion store and buy a lion seed and grow a lion from a pot! . . . Wow! I was *off!* Now I don't have four-year-olds around anymore—maybe I'll make up stories for grandchildren one day—but there's a permanent four-year-old in my head, to whom I tell my stories. I've worked on three in the last year, but none is any good. If you have the proper shape, the *fable*, maybe they're not so hard to write— economy, limits of diction, right details . . . but finding the fable is hard! For each of my juveniles, the publisher found the illustrator, asking my approval; then the illustrator has asked me questions, maybe shown me samples. I've been fortunate: Barbara Cooney, Mary Azarian.

Does the war of the anthologies (yours, Pack's, and Simpsons's versus Donald Allen's anthology) stay with you to this day (even though you included the work of Ginsberg, Snyder, and others in a later anthology you edited for Penguin)? What Young Turks have you lived to see become deacons?

The war of the anthologies was real enough, back at the end of the fifties. For some nostalgic and sentimental people it still goes on. *Ah, the barricades!* These aging Beatniks remind me of people in my parents' generation who lived out their lives in nostalgia over Prohibition. Bathtub gin! Speakeasies! . . . I speak without disinterest, because I am still loathed here and there as a leader of the Eastern Establishment, Mr. Hallpack

Simpson, Enemy, Archbishop of Academic Poetry! . . . People want to relive their youths, when good was good and bad was stanzas.

For the most part good poets want no part of it. Creeley and I, Ginsberg and I, were famous enemies . . . but we stopped that stuff twenty-five years ago. In 1961 Denise Levertov, who was poetry editor at the *Nation*, asked me to review Charles Olson's first volume of *The Maximus Poems*. Ecumenism was already with us. In 1962 I did my Penguin with Levertov, Creeley, and Snyder, only five years after Hallpack. (Five years is a long time when it starts in your twenties.) By 1961 I was abashed by the rigidity that defended my citadel when I was in my mid-twenties.

I don't think that *particular* war endures except for nostalgic diehards—but there will always be outs and ins; and the first shall be last: sometimes. I see geographical complacency and enmity now. What is a Los Angeles poem? (I don't think there's a New Hampshire poem.) For the most part, geographical groups are diffident folk trying to build castles to feel safe in. To hell with it. I want to be a poet by myself, not a New England poet or a deep image poet or what have you. In my own generation in America, the poet I admire the most is not considered a member of my gang. Robert Creeley.

Those anthologies provided a dialectic for their time. Does such a dialectic exist now, or is it a time for synthesis, revision, mannerism, or utter impasse? Was the aesthetic distance between your and Allen's anthology a real one? Are you ever tempted to edit another anthology of younger poets at your age?

I've been asked to edit an anthology of the young and I have refused. Let the young edit the young. I could do it—but the passion would not be there, and if I made fewer gross mistakes the whole thing would be a big mistake. I don't like recent anthologies of younger poets because they are too damned big. Out of generosity or whatever, probably whatever, they include too many aspirants and contribute to the confusion of numbers.

I don't really think there's a dialectic now though it seems so to some. Metrical poets against the world. Free-verse plain talk poets against the world. Language Poets against the world. Narrative poets against the world. There's a comfort in being *out*, and people warm themselves by that cold fire. But conflict *does* make energy. Maybe it's a time of warring tribes, Balkanization, rather than a time of dueling superpowers. Oh, it wasn't really superpowers ever, not even back then . . . Allen Ginsberg, Frank O'Hara, Robert Duncan, Denise Levertov, and John Ashbery did not resemble each other.

What's good about growing older?

What's bad about growing older is the knowledge that you have less *time*, the frustration that you will not live to write the books or the poems; or to read all the books you want to. What is good, paradoxically enough, is patience. With less time I feel or act as if I had more. When I begin a poem of any ambition, I know that I will be working on it five years from now; I *sigh* a little . . . but I get on with it. I feel more energy, need less sleep, feel more excitement about work than I did when I was thirty or forty. I've been lucky in my second marriage, in living where I want to live; these are not inevitable results of aging.

Simpson says he has scolded you for writing so much about the business of poetry—the number of books sold, number of readings, etc. What do you think about that? (Rexroth also wrote of these matters, yes?)

Louis and I fight about lots of things. He was outraged when I wrote an article about poetry readings. I write essays in poetic theory, and essays of appreciation, but from time to time I write essays of fact. I am interested, for example, in how writers make their livings; I always liked *New Grub Street,* and biographies. Think of Emerson making his living by traveling around the country, at first by steamer and stagecoach, lecturing week after week—like Robert Bly. As for numbers: It annoys the hell out of me that people generalize, as if the facts were common knowledge, when they don't know the facts. One constantly hears how poetry sells less than it ever did;

even publishers say so. But the numbers show something different. Now *numbers* don't necessarily have anything to do with quality—I grant Louis that—but let's find out what the facts are before we generalize about them! I'm curious about the sociology of poetry: If poets typically make a living as teachers, is their workday unrelated to the poetry that they write? I used to be fascinated by all the English poets who lived by their wits freelancing. A couple of centuries ago a good many were vicars. The poetry reading must explain a great deal—good and bad—about the kind of poetry that is written today. There is also the phenomenon of the creative writing industry.

What do you think accounts for the dearth of polemics in current writings about poetics? Compared to Pound and Lewis's Blast, *or Bly's* The Fifties, *why do we see so few picking up the cudgel these days? Is it part of an "I'm okay; you're okay" relativism and "Make Nice" culture, or just a period of exhaustion, politeness, or fear?*

Compare the reviews in English magazines! Nastiness is a dumb convention over there as our namby-pambyness is a dumb convention here. "Boost don't knock," said the Boosters Club. How many poets have you heard say that they don't want to review anything unless they can praise it? Oh, I don't believe in taking a cannon to kill a flea. It's a waste of time to write a savage review of a book that nobody is going to read. But I believe in taking a cannon to kill a flea continually described as an eagle. I've tried to do it once or twice.

What do you think about creative writing programs being separated from English departments and being put under the aegis, say, of a fine arts department, along with dancers, musicians, theater people?

Separating creative writing from the regular English department is a disaster. "Here are the people who can read; here are the people who can write. People who can write can't read; people who can read can't write." Wonderful. Specialization is a curse, especially for poets. Separate departments divide old poetry from new. Some places have literature departments *within* creative writing departments, where writers teach reading to would-be writers. But the value of writers to English departments lies not in the teaching of creative writing; it's their teaching of literature classes for regular undergraduates or graduates. Of course most Ph.D.'s are dopes; so are most poets. Undergraduate English majors—or engineers and nurses taking an elective—suffer because they never get to be taught by a writer. The faculty suffers because separations make for complacency; nobody's challenging you with an alternative. But the teacher of creative writing suffers most. When you teach literature you spend your days with great work—reading it, talking about it, reading papers about it. Great literature rubs off and you *learn* by teaching, by encountering what you don't know well enough, teaching it to people who know it even less.

This separation makes for narcissism, complacency, and ignorance. It's the worst thing that has happened with the creative writing industry. People spend their whole lives talking about line-breaks and the *New Yorker.*

But why should poets teach literature rather than conduct writing workshops?

If you teach great literature you live among the great models. You make your living reading Moore and Pound and Hardy and Marvell and Yeats! Incredible. Students ask you questions, and when you answer you discover that you knew something you didn't know you knew. Instead of living with half-baked first drafts by narcissistic teenagers, you live with the *greatest art.* What could be a better way to spend your spare time—when you're not competing directly with Wordsworth—than by reading Wordsworth?

The first readers for your poems—Bly, Kinnell, Simpson, Bidart, Orr, and others—how have their readings changed and developed over time?

Jane Kenyon is my first reader and has been for fifteen years. Robert Bly has read virtually every poem I've written for forty years. Simpson, Snodgrass, Kinnell . . . these people have helped me enormously through the years. For a while in our twenties Adrienne Rich and I worked on each other's poems. When we lived near each other, Gregory Orr helped me. I haven't known Frank Bidart so long but he has been extremely helpful; Robert Pinsky on occasion, Wendell Berry very often. Bly's reading has changed the most. He used to cut and rewrite; sometimes I took his corrections and put them in print: More often they showed me what was wrong and therefore helped me toward my own changes. More recently he has taken to speaking more about the underneath of the poem, touching the text less. Galway is a marvelous editor, a great cutter. Snodgrass is superb at a Johnsonian reading, following syntax and implication, allowing himself to be puzzled.

What goes into your choosing someone to be such a reader of your work? Their ability to argue their position? You said in an Iowa Review *interview with David Hamilton that the criticism of younger writers has not been of much use to you. Why is that?*

I don't choose anybody. We choose each other—a mating dance, tentative advances and retreats. Criticism *must* be mutual, a dialogue. It doesn't work so well when criticism goes in one direction only. And the poetics has to have something in common; if two people are simply opposed, there's no common ground where conversation can happen. And it helps to get your own notions thrown back at you when you violate them. Within a general agreement, then you should be as different as possible—like Bly and me.

The requirements are more temperamental than generational. Since that interview with David Hamilton, I have made great use of some young readers (young compared to me). With some young poets, you sense that they may be frightened, or deferential, or counterdeferential, which is just as bad—acting nastier than they feel, in order to show that they're not cowed. When I answered Hamilton, I was thinking of some dreadful examples of young fans praising elderly slop; the young were sincere but dazzled. I don't forgive the old for believing what they want to believe.

You're one of the few writers your age I know who still reads and comments on the work of younger writers, aside from people who formally teach or are busy writing blurbs. Most writers, once they reach fifty or so, confine themselves to reading the work of their own generation and work of the distant past. Why has this been different for you?

I keep looking. I'm *curious:* What's happening? What's going to happen? I've seen nothing so extraordinary as the increased *numbers* of poets, people with at least some ability; the numbers especially of young women, compared to earlier generations, including mine. Because I was so rigid when I was young, I try to stay open to kinds of poetry alien to my own; of course openness can become a mindless relativism or namby-pambyness. You have to worry: Do I just want them to *like* me? One thing I learned ten or twenty years ago: If you read something that upsets you, that violates every canon you ever considered . . . look again, look harder. It might be *poetry.* This notion helped me read Frank Bidart. I read the Language Poets without great success, but some please me more than others: Perelman, Palmer, Hejinian, Silliman.

You can't keep up forever. I look into as many as six hundred new books a year. I'm not telling you that I read every poem; I get tired. Like everybody else I get tired reading the same poem over and over again, but it's not only that. When I was in my twenties Richard Eberhart, who was only fifty, told me that he could no longer tell the young apart. He was not being insulting; he was complaining, not bragging. I suppose it happens to everyone. Maybe it begins to happen to me; but I remain avid to *keep up.* I suppose the feeling is more acquisitive than altruistic, but from time to time I can help someone. On the other hand, I continually get book-length manuscripts by mail from strangers, usually wanting me to find them a publisher. I cannot even read them all. Too much!

Could you speak a bit about your processes of revision?

I'm not quick. So many things have looked good and in retrospect were awful! I need to keep things around a long time; if

I keep staring, I find out what's wrong. Or I think I do. Usually it takes years of staring, until I take them inside me; sometimes I wake up at night with a problem about a poem, or a solution to a problem, when I have not seen the poem for a year or more. Mostly I work on poems every day for months; then I get fed up and put them away; then I find myself obsessing about them again and drag them out and get to work.

I must say, I enjoy revising! It's the best kind of work. The initial inspiration is over quickly, scary and manic; then I love the daily work, the struggle with language and the sweet difficulty of that struggle!

Your work as an editor for the Harvard Advocate, *the* Paris Review, *the Wesleyan poetry series, Harper and Row, the University of Michigan series, and* Harvard Magazine—*how has this affected your life? What advice might you have for editors, for a long life spent tending to the work of other poets?*

When you edit you impose your own taste. Especially when I was younger and passionate about the work of my own generation, I wanted to impose my taste on *everybody*. Of course at this point I no longer agree with my old taste, but I don't disavow the motive. Other editors worked with a countertaste. Conflict makes energy, and I'm all for it. I started the Poets on Poetry series with the University of Michigan Press because I wanted to be able to read the books. I'd read an article here and there by this poet or that, but when I wanted to lay my hands on an essay I couldn't find it. I made the series in order to preserve fugitive and miscellaneous pieces—interviews, book reviews, full dress articles, what have you.

Advice: Never edit by committee! Advocate, disparage, make public what you love and what you hate! When you stop loving and hating, stop editing.

The Michigan series, Poets on Poetry—Robert McDowell said in a review of the series that "The Mum Was Always Talking." I have the suspicion, along with McDowell, that if this series were not done we would have precious little record of the poetics of your generation. Did growing up, coming to fruition in the shadow of the New Critics inhibit poets from writing prose about their poetry, from writing any kind of criticism at all? W. S. Merwin once said it had that effect on him.

Yes, many of us felt the way Merwin speaks of. You had a feeling that some older poets would *rather* write an essay than a poem! And we reacted. Now there's a further reaction, parallel to and symptomatic of the separation of the English department from creative writing, which says that if you think about poetry—or utter thoughts about it, or allude to any poet born before 1925—you're a pedant. Bah!

How long did you write textbooks before you could count on any royalties from them as a basis for your income as a freelance writer?

When I quit teaching I had no confidence that my income was great enough to support my family, with my children going to college. At that time *Writing Well* made more money for me than any other book but I couldn't count on it. Really, it hasn't been textbooks that have supported us. My income derives from such a variety of sources—textbooks, juveniles, trade books (many old things bring in a pittance every year), poetry readings, magazine sales . . . *Writing Well* doesn't sell so well as it used to; other textbooks help but I don't rely on them. The many sources do a couple of things. They provide extraordinary variety in the work I do; and they have the virtues of a multiple conglomerate: If one sort of writing dwindles—if I lose interest or the market crumbles or my ability diminishes within a genre—there's something else to pick it up. Of course, these advantages are accidental; I didn't become so various on purpose. I always take pleasure in trying something new.

Bly looks at the world as a Jungian and you as a Freudian. How has Freud affected your view of things? What have the insights of psychology, and psychoanalysis in particular, meant to you and your generation of poets?

I started reading Freud in 1953. Ten years later I started psychotherapy with a Freudian analyst, the only analyst in Ann Arbor who would do therapy. Reading Freud was exciting and gave me ideas. I could have found much the same in Heraclitus: Whenever somebody shows you north, suspect south. Later, the experience of therapy was profound. It touches me every day and it goes *with* poetry rather than *against* it. You learn to release, to allow the ants—and the butterflies—to come out from under the rock; but first you have to know the rock's there! The names of the creatures that scramble out are up to you. Psychotherapy properly is never a matter of the *explanations* of feelings, nor of "Eureka!" as in Hollywood. It is a transforming thing. It makes your skin alert; it builds a system of sensors. Not censors! Jung, on the other hand, seems a mildly interesting literary figure, full of fascinating ideas and disgusting ones mixed together with more regard for color than for truth. Freud is as nasty as the world is, as human life is. Jung is decorative. Freud is the streets and Jung is a Fourth of July parade through the streets, a parade of minor deities escaped from the zoo of polytheism. Freud the atheist has the relentlessness of monotheism.

Will you ever write an autobiography of your adult life?

No.

How do you work up a biography?

You work on a biography by interviewing everybody and reading everything and taking notes and keeping files and taking a deep breath and plunging in. Of course biography is fiction. Again and again you have to make choices because your information contradicts itself. Did it happen this way or that way? Hell, you have to make the same choices writing out of your own life! You remember something with perfect clarity and you're perfectly wrong. How can we expect that biography be true? Mind you, it is not the same as writing a novel; there are *certain* scruples.

54

Who, aside from writers, have been your most important teachers?

Henry Moore. I spent a good deal of time with him, talking with him, watching him work. He had the most wonderful attitude toward work and his art. He was interested only in being better than Michelangelo, and he knew he could never achieve it; so he got up every morning and tried again. He was a gregarious man who learned to forgo companionship for the sake of work. He knew what he had to do. He remained decent to others, although it is difficult; people make it difficult for you when you're that damned famous. He knew the difference between putting in time—you can work sixteen hours a day and remain lazy—and really working as an artist, trying to *break through.*

How would you place your poems among the poems of the past? I'm thinking here of Keats's statement, which you mentioned in "Poetry and Ambition," that "I would sooner fail, than not be among the greatest." You've also wisely said that we are bad at judging our work—we either think too much of it or too little of it.

I can't place my poems among the poems of the past and I doubt the sanity or the intelligence of people who say that they can. When Keats said that he would "sooner fail than not be among the greatest," note that he did not tell us that he *was* among the greatest. He *wishes* to be among the English poets when he is dead; he does not tell us that he already *is*. When I was young I had the illusion that at some point or other you would *know* if you were good. I no longer believe that such knowledge is possible. Some days you feel you're terrific; some days you feel that you're crap. So what? Get on with it.

You have said that during the time The Alligator Bride *and* The Town of Hill *were published, you were floundering as a writer, conscious that nothing you did was as good as some earlier poems. Why did you publish the poems of that period?*

It was from 1969 to 1975 that I floundered; *The Alligator Bride* came out in 1969 and included "The Man in the Dead Machine," which I thought (and still think) was as good as anything I had done up to then. Also, I liked the title poem and several other new things—but after *The Alligator*, for six years, I felt that nothing that I was doing was as good as what I had done. I didn't think that what I was writing was beneath contempt; it's melancholy enough to think that nothing was as good as "The Man in the Dead Machine." I like the title poem of *The Town of Hill* better than anything else out of that patch. I published these poems because I thought that they were good . . . (I've often been wrong; I've published many poems in magazines that I later left out of books; in the old *New Yorker* anthology, half my poems weren't good enough to put into a book.) Also I published to cheer myself up in a bad time, an ignoble reason but maybe effective. *The Town of Hill* is not my best work, but when Godine bought it I was released into the long line of "Kicking the Leaves." If I had not rid the house of those floundering poems, I'm not sure I could have written the new ones.

The One Day works with the kind of "multiple protagonist" voice we find in "The Waste Land." Why did you make this choice, rather than stay in the fairly monolyrical voice which had characterized much of your work?

Picasso said that every human being is a colony. An old friend of mine said that she was not a person but ran a boarding-house. One of the many problems with the "monolyrical" is that it pretends that each of us is singular.

Your work is your church. Have you always been Christian? How does being a Christian enter into your work? Isn't the absence of a god (or gods) or an agnosticism an important part of much contemporary poetry? How do you see your work amidst that? If it is something you shy from speaking of, why do you shy from it? Better left unsaid, bad manners, or just refusing to talk about politics and religion at the dinner table?

I was brought up a Christian, suburban Protestant variety. When I was twelve I converted myself to atheism. During the years I spent in the English village of Thaxted, I used to go to church every Sunday, telling myself that I went because the carving and architecture were so beautiful, because I loved the vicar (high church and a Communist), because the ceremony was beautiful . . . Now I think I was kidding myself in saying that my feelings were aesthetic. Yes, I am shy of speaking about it. The figure of Jesus is incredibly important, the astonishing figure from the Gospels. I used to think that people who went to church were either swallowing everything or pretending to, hypocritically. Now I know that intelligent practicing Christians often feel total spiritual drought and disbelief; still, even in such moments, ancient ritual and story can be entered, practiced, listened to, considered . . .

Not too long ago you did a review of small literary presses for Iowa Review. John Hollander has said that when he was first publishing you could count on a few of the elders to let you know what kind of noises your work was making. Very few older writers now review the work of younger writers, or emerging presses, except to write blurbs for them. Why is this? What is your "policy" about writing blurbs, and why?

Thirty years ago I was asked to write blurbs for a few books. I was flattered to be asked, and wrote the blurbs. When the books came out I looked like an ass. Then I looked at other people's blurbs; *they* looked like asses. There are some *honorable* people's blurbs, and even *they* looked like asses. There are exceptions, but almost every blurb is foolish. The formula for a blurb is an adjective, an adverb, and a verb that usually combine opposites. X is both free-swinging and utterly orderly; Y is classic and romantic; Z is high and at the same time, amazingly, low. Many book reviewers review blurbs rather than the poetry. Blurbs are the Good Housekeeping Seal of Approval. I think it's far worse in poetry than it is in fiction. Although doubtless many poets write blurbs out of generosity, it doesn't look that way; it gives vent to the widespread notion that poets live by taking each other's laundry. Blurbs hurt poetry. They are done because publishers are too lazy to name what they're printing. Almost always, it would be better to print a poem or an excerpt from a poem . . . but, oh, these terrible blurbs. I refuse to do it.

Although I've refused 12,457 times, although I've written essays against the practice, I still receive two hundred and fifty or three hundred requests a year to write blurbs. How could I add three hundred books and three hundred mini-essays to my life every year? This is *not* my reason for refusing to do them, but it would be reason enough. When publishers quote from reviews, excerpts from journalistic occasions, nobody can stop them. Blurbs are *pseudo*-reviews, and they appear to be used in lieu of dinner invitations, thank-you letters, and gold stars. They're repellent, fulsome, and rebarbative.

Reviewing is in terrible shape. There's more poetry than ever—more readings, more books, more *sales* of books—and less reviewing. And worse reviewing. Literary journalists like Malcolm Cowley, Louise Bogan, and Edmund Wilson made their living, in large part, by writing book reviews. Their descendants have tenure instead and teach Linebreaks 101. The *New Yorker,* by appointing Helen Vendler, resigned from reviewing poetry. *Atlantic* and *Harper's* and the old *Saturday Review* reviewed poetry; no more. The *New York Review of Books* isn't interested in poetry and becomes stupid when it pretends to. The *New York Times* is at its worst on poetry. What's left? The *New Republic* and the *Nation* are honorable; there are the quarterlies, each of them read by twelve people. *APR* reviews little. We suffer from a lack of intelligent *talk* about poetry. I don't know why. Maybe it's the same cultural separatism that splits creative writing and literature in the university, an epidemic of ignorance, willful know-nothingism. When Vendler is the leading critic of contemporary poetry we're in a bad way. She can write a sentence but she has *no taste.* She's a bobbysoxer for poets she swoons over: some good, some bad; she can't tell the difference.

You went to Harvard with Ashbery, Bly, O'Hara, Koch, Rich, Davison, and others. You dated Adrienne Rich. More to say on The Poet's Theatre, as it started there?

Harvard from 1947 to 1951 was a lively place. There was a wonderful independent theater group down at the Brattle. We started the Poet's Theatre out of the coincidence of theatrical and poetic activity, and the momentary ascendancy of poor old Christopher Fry; of course Eliot worked at poetic drama. The Poet's Theatre never produced anything memorable but it was a center where energy gathered.

At the *Advocate* we sat around and argued all night. Koch, Ashbery, Bly. O'Hara was around, and Rich. Bly became my best friend. He and I double dated, with Rich my date. I think Adrienne and I went out twice. At least once I was *awful:* I got pissed and argued with Bly, showing off. Adrienne was *polite.* Much later, when I was married and at Oxford and she was living there as a Guggenheim Fellow, we got to be best friends, very close. I feel gratitude to her, and affection . . . Bly remains my best friend. O'Hara and I were friends for a while, then we quarreled over something or other. He was wonderfully funny and alert and lively, a nifty spirit. Ashbery was intelligent and quiet and smart and talented. It was a good time. We competed, you might say.

You've championed the work of poets as different as Robert Creeley and <u>Geoffrey Hill</u>. What accounts for the catholicity of your taste?

Sometimes I fear that my catholicity is another name for mindlessness . . . but I don't *really* think so. I like to say things like, "If you can't admire both Hill and Creeley, you can't read poetry." (That isn't true either.) Hell, Creeley resembles nobody so much as Henry James. Hill makes the tensest language in the universe, with more sparks flying between adjacent words than any other poet since Andrew Marvell. Both are geniuses. Of course they can't read each other. Vendler can't read either of them.

Who do you think of now as the most interesting men or women of letters? Do you think the person of letters is a kind of vanishing beast?

People have been talking about the disappearance of the Man of Letters ever since Uncle Matthew died. People resurrect the phrase when they want to praise somebody who writes more than one thing: Edmund Wilson, Lionel Trilling. But we have candidates even now: Sven Birkerts writes essays about reading, writes essays about poetry . . . Lately, many younger poets in America, male and female, spread out by doing other writing as well as poetry—fiction, essays, criticism. *Good!* You learn about your primary art by practicing or investigating other arts—especially others that use language. Now "man of letters" is a fine phrase but it would be a pompous label to put on yourself. Instead, you can call yourself a literary journalist. (Maybe when you're eighty you can call yourself a man or woman of letters.) Let writers come out from under the Rock of the University of America! Let them stick their noses under the rock of the buggy world! Let them make a living by writing.

How do you avoid the whining and the bitterness?

Well, to start with, I whine bitterly a whole lot . . . Whining and bitterness *are* a waste of time and spirit, and they hurt—reason enough to avoid them. You feel bitter about trivial things: *They* have left you out of the Final Anthology—the last bus to the Immortality Graveyard. Or: Everybody *else* gets this prize.

There are things I try to remember, things that help: *All prizes are rubber medals.* All grapes are sour as soon as you taste them. I haven't won the Pulitzer; if I ever win it, within five minutes I will recollect all the dopes, idiots, time-servers, and class-presidents of poetry who have won the Pulitzer; I will know that getting the Pulitzer means that I'm no damned good. Needless to say, I still want to undergo this humiliation!

Also, it matters to remember: *You're never going to know whether you're good.* Nothing in the inside world stays secure. Nothing in the outside world—like three Nobels for literature in a row, retiring the trophy; like the sale of one million copies of your collected poems in two weeks; like effigies of your person selling in Walmarts from coast to coast—will convince you that you're any damned good. So: Give up the notion. What's left? What's left is work.

Of course you still feel annoyance and anger when you're abused. When somebody says something nasty, you can't get the tune out of your head. Words burn themselves into your brain the way an electric needle burns a slogan onto pine; you etch-a-sketch the unforgivable words onto your skull. It would be good not to read reviews but it's impossible, because if a critic gets nasty there's someone out there who'll xerox the worst parts and mail them to you. The emperor was right to execute the messenger.

But . . . I know so many aging poets, who ream their brains out with rage over mistreatment, neglect, slights both imagined and true. A terrible thing to watch! Because I've seen it so much, I expend energy fending rage off—whining and bitterness—within myself, explaining to myself, over and over again, how the reputation stock market rises and falls as irrationally as Wall Street does; remembering literary history and all the *famous* poets no one has heard of; reminding myself: *Get back to the desk.*

Eliot At One Hundred

1. Waiting for Eliot

Pound's Sextus wearily proclaims, "I shall have, doubtless, a boom after my funeral, / Seeing that longstanding increases all things"; and he adds with prophylactic irony, "regardless of quality."

But reputation's rabbit bolts for unpredictable holes, and the vagaries of public love—on which poets alive waste so much bitter meditation—continue their wandering after the funeral. Forty and fifty years back, Eliot's preeminence was unquestionable. Perhaps in reaction, the critical eminences of our moment dismiss his poems. Eliot's own announcement of a secure minority, which once exhibited modesty's charm, comes to seem a disputed boast. William Carlos Williams's revenge is sweet—or, rather, the revenge of Eliot's less public enemy Wallace Stevens, because it is Stevens's reputation that has replaced Eliot's. Now we study phenomenology rather than Anglicanism and quote Hartford à la française instead of a London/Missouri patois.

Wallace Stevens made beautiful poems; and it is not necessary to Choose One of the Above. But the contrast is instructive. Eliot—like Pound, Joyce, and Yeats—is deeply historical. In their historicism the English-language modernists differed from the generally expressionist modernists of the Interna-

---

The first note appeared in the *Southern Review* in 1988; the review of Eliot's letters came out in the Boston *Globe* the same year.

tional Style. Our own literary era remains shallow from lack of history. This levity afflicts not only undergraduates but professors. Wallace Stevens is ahistorical, nowhere more clearly than when he hints at historicism, as in "Sunday Morning." On the other hand, Eliot's eventually-Christian mysticism, his out-of-time travel, which perceives the simultaneous coexistence of all cultures and events, becomes possible only to the historical imagination. Readers lacking an historical sense will remain unable to read Eliot—not to mention Pound, Joyce, and Yeats; not to mention Jones and Hill.

In the matter of Eliot we flatter our rejection of history by calling it a denial of Eliot's social, political, and religious ideas. But without a countersense (of history), such rejection is sentimental. Eliot is more ambitious, or more ambitious in the way of Dante, than any other English-language modernist bar Pound. He waits for us again when we are ready for him. When younger poets return to Eliot as a source, they will find in his work everything necessary to great ambition. In his learning combined with imagination, he provides the double model of maker and seer. His sensuousness of sound (the Bloomsbury mask disguises it for some readers) is as luscious as Pound's or Stevens's: take "Marina"; take that journey of poetry and spirit, "Ash Wednesday."

Although he could make the small perfected lyric—"Journey of the Magi" is intelligent, stately, and conclusive—he could also do something more difficult. In *The Waste Land,* he resolved (with Pound's help) an extraordinary manyness or diversity, deeply historical and deeply psychic. Neither Stevens nor Williams nor Frost ever attempted such diversity in a single poem—cities and centuries, huge swings of spirit. (Pound's most ambitious endeavors take him past the *possibility* of resolution.) Later, in *Four Quartets* at its best, Eliot's historical intelligence and formal mastery make great poetry again out of ambitious diversity. The terza rima passage of "Little Gidding" (learning and wisdom, Dante and a human life) is literature as magnificent as anyone has made for two hundred years. Maybe we need not wait on Eliot forever.

2. The Young Man in His Letters

Monarchist from Missouri, prophet of the waste land, Anglo-Catholic communicant, T. S. Eliot was born a hundred years ago in Saint Louis. Publication of the first volume of his letters provides one or two surprises. In 1921 this solemn dark-suited fellow—who worked in a bank, who wrote starchy prose for the *Times Literary Supplement,* who in his public persona resembled a rolled umbrella—ended a letter to Ezra Pound, "Good fucking, brother." In my informal obscenity index, I find elsewhere several occasions of "shit" and a nice allusion to "bovine excreta." The jovial Latinity is more predictable.

It is a pleasure to read these letters, as they reveal the young Eliot for good and ill. At least, it is a pleasure for those of us who care for the man and his work. This heavy volume of letters, enriched with poignant photographs, gives us the material by which we begin to create our own Eliot. We are told that three further volumes will follow this one. Here we find a few early letters, and then a great accumulation from Oxford through the London of 1922, a period that contains the central episode of Eliot's life—when he married Vivienne and became a poet instead of a professor—and concludes with *The Waste Land.*

But we are disappointed if we expect to hear Eliot speak directly about his poetry. He refers to a long poem, which he hopes to find time to write, which turned out to be *The Waste Land,* but he never speaks of his poetic intentions. He saves intentions for their expression in poems. Mostly, these letters are hasty and obligatory, written in fatigue after a day at the bank and a night writing articles for magazines or editing. They become more consequential when they take up literary business, as Eliot begins to edit the *Criterion.*

This volume belongs on the Eliot shelf, not on the shelf of great letter writers. He was an affectionate man, close to family and to friends, but he did not devote himself to the literary form of the letter the way the greatest letter writers do. Among Americans, I mean Henry James, Eliot's mid-Atlantic predecessor, and Henry Adams, his distant cousin. Eliot lacked leisure or energy for great letters because he worked long hours, came home from the bank to a sick wife, and stayed up late writing reviews, articles, and lectures in order to meet medical expenses. Which is not to make Vivienne a villain. She lives at the center of this book, and indeed at the center of Eliot's life and work. Although the marriage was miserable for both people, if we cherish the poetry we must be grateful to the marriage and to Vivienne; for Vivienne sponsored and encouraged the poet. The marriage was sudden and impulsive, repented at leisure, but the impulse was consciously connected with the choice of poetry over professorship. Eliot's mother and father had promoted the academy at the expense of poetry, wishing to sire a Professor of Philosophy rather than a practitioner of—we can see parental noses wrinkle—*vers libre*. The sexually immature Eliot, meeting this attractive, zany, intuitive young woman just before he expected to undertake a life without poetry, married her at a registry office and cabled his family. He chose poetry, anxiety, and sex over tenure and the faculty club.

A strength of this book is its inclusion of many letters from Eliot's circle: his parents, Pound, Russell, and above all Vivienne. We begin to know Vivienne. It is inevitable that we compare her to Zelda Fitzgerald, who also wanted to become a dancer, who also attempted writing and drawing, who was an artist *manqué*, who was both stimulating and destructive. Vivienne was vivacious when she was not depressed; she was a mimic with an observant ear; she was kind, loony, supportive, and insupportable. Eliot's letters become bulletins of Vivienne's illness: "Vivienne is wretched today—another bad night." He writes Bertrand Russell, "We went to the dentist this afternoon . . . She is very low tonight." But Vivienne's letters are more telling. She often wrote her mother-in-law, providing just the news you want to hear about your distant youngest son: "most gloomy and depressed and very irritable and I knew he felt that life was simply not worth going on with." "Life rushes by—with us. Somehow it all seems a long scramble, an *effort*, and one scarcely has time to think. A good thing, perhaps. Please excuse pencil." To her brother-in-law, she typically writes, "I arrived here yesterday. I hate it. It is poisonous. I shall leave as soon as I decently can." In her staccato hysteria one recognizes the nervous syntax of *The Waste Land*. When in this collection of letters we encounter Eliot's own nervous breakdown, he seems to imitate Vivienne, as if they briefly exchanged seats on the seesaw. Yet she is uncannily a source for his art: we understand that her lively intuition opened a door by which poetry entered, and when Eliot finishes *The Waste Land,* he writes a friend that he "must wait for [Vivienne's] opinion as to whether it is printable." We never doubt it.

Some of the letters written by others might as well be Eliot's. Especially when he was younger, Eliot enlisted others to argue his cause. When he married, he had Ezra Pound write his father—an intelligent, conventional businessman of St. Louis—a letter advocating poetry, which dropped hints that the Eliot family might support their poet the way the Pound family supported theirs. Later Bertrand Russell wrote letters in Eliot's support to St. Louis, when the senior Eliots were urging their son to cross the Atlantic for his Ph.D. orals; German submarines were on the prowl, and Russell's cable suggested that possibly the Ph.D. was not worth drowning for.

Friendships are crucial to volumes of letters. When Eliot first mentions Ezra Pound in a letter to Conrad Aiken, he calls Pound's verses "touchingly incompetent," a judgment he turned upside down. In a later letter to Pound, he calls Aiken "stupid." He was annoyed, because Aiken as poet had fallen into imitation of him; Eliot described Aiken's new style, accurately enough, as a compound of Swinburne and himself. There is an exchange with Richard Aldington which shows Eliot at a height of disinterest, for Aldington at the beginning of the correspondence (with equal probity) let Eliot understand he *loathed* Eliot's verses. Because they respected each other's intelligence, the friendship thrived—until Eliot made mild criticism of some prose sentences by Aldington and suggested revisions. It was as inevitable as sunrise that Aldington flew into a rage. Of course the correspondence with Pound— or the friendship that sponsored it—engages the center of modern literature.

Reading the first volume of Eliot's letters, we begin to construct his biography—as we watch him fabricate his public persona. Forty and fifty years ago he made a frightening figure. We find in these letters a predictable distinction between "Tom" and "T. S. Eliot." In letters to friends he is affectionate, lighthearted, even cheerfully obscene as he was to Pound. Constructing the ironies of a letter to the editor, or dropping a remark about Edmund Gosse, he can be fierce. I am reminded of the eminent baseballist Sandy Koufax who described pitching as the art of intimidation. If you want to become literary dictator—and why not?—cultivate a mix of austerity and asperity. It worked well for a man born a century ago in Saint Louis.

In Roethke's House

The Glass House is a writer's book—the work of a novelist, devoted to literature and its craft, writing about a dead friend who was a poet. Theodore Roethke and Allan Seager were graduated from the University of Michigan a year apart. At that time, they scarcely knew each other, but their coincidence allows Seager to sketch out of memory the ambience of Roethke's Michigan. A decade later, when they had both started to publish, they met again at a writer's conference and became friends. Roethke suggested that Seager join him at Bennington College in Vermont, where they spent one year teaching together. They remained close until Roethke died at fifty-five in 1963. Allan Seager died five years later, at sixty-two, and this biography of his friend was his last work.

It was my luck to know both men. I knew Roethke only slightly, but for ten years I taught at the University of Michigan with Allan Seager. He was my senior by twenty years, and I had begun to read him in adolescence, saving my allowance when I was fourteen to buy his first novel, *Equinox*. Probably Seager's best novels were *Amos Berry* and *Hilda Manning;* there was also a fine book of short stories called *The Old Man of the Mountain*. (Eight of the stories had turned up in annual Best collections.) Seager's fiction was highly praised by Hugh Kenner, James Dickey, Robert Penn Warren . . . but it never won general recognition. Today one novel remains in print.

An introduction to Allan Seager's biography of Theodore Roethke, *The Glass House*, as reissued by the University of Michigan Press, 1991.

Allan considered us an embattled pair, as writers who were faculty members at the University of Michigan. We were Practitioners of the Word, islanded in a sea of Ph.D.'s who could not write an office-hours schedule without stylistic infelicity. Allan exaggerated; Allan enjoyed exaggerating. An erect, handsome, ironic figure, he strode the corridors of Haven Hall, where the English department pastured itself, and popped his head into my office to tell a story: to quote a colleague's latest gaffe; to pass on writerly gossip. He told me stories about his friend Ted Roethke—whose work I had long admired—as cautionary tales or exemplary anecdotes for the edification of an apprentice. He spoke with affection about Ted's eccentricities, ambitions, habits of work—especially about Ted's professionalism, as we might have called it if Roethke had not been a poet.

When I was an undergraduate, I ran across Theodore Roethke's *The Lost Son* and was immediately enthralled. After graduation, doing some time at Oxford in 1951, I lectured at the Poetry Society on "New American Poets"; I dwelt upon Lowell, Wilbur, and Roethke. Later I wrote a two-part piece for a magazine in London telling about "American Poets Since the War" and praised Roethke again. During a brief stint at Stanford a year later, when I published a poem in a quarterly, Roethke telephoned from Seattle to congratulate me. (He knew I admired his work; he wanted to like mine.) He telephoned in December of 1953, while I was out Christmas shopping, and talked to my wife, telling her that he wanted to bring me to Seattle for a poetry reading—which was an absurd notion: I had published only two poems in American magazines, and no books. What else he said, I don't know, but he talked for an hour with enthusiasm and high excitement; much later, I learned that Roethke called from a hospital— and I understood the blood chemistry of his enthusiasm. Ignorant in 1953, I wrote him a note about the putative poetry reading, and a month later he answered that the university was out of funds; as for his own, "the Aga Khan phase is over for this year." In the spring of 1954 I heard him read at San Francisco State's Poetry Center—an ingratiating powerhouse of a reading, heavy on comic routines—and talked with him at a reception the next day. It was nine years before I saw him a second and last time.

Allan and his friend were men of their generation, courtly or flirtatious with women and cronyish with men, Prohibition-generation drinkers, funny, and decent; these two committed their lives to literature. Although Roethke was a poet, he aspired to the status of a professional writer—like Allan who had edited at *Vanity Fair* when he was a young man, who wrote serious novels and supported them by stories in the *Saturday Evening Post*. Not all poets want to be *writers*—not Shelley, not Blake, not Rilke—but a few poets have been professional workers in literature, not above supporting themselves by the pen: among others, Jonson, Dryden, Johnson, Hardy, Lawrence, Plath. Suffering from the delusion that fiction paid, Roethke collected books of advice on how to write it. Doubtless, like Sylvia Plath, he looked into *Writers' Digest* from time to time; one cannot imagine Rainer Maria Rilke poring over *WD*'s list of poetry markets.

But of course poetry for Roethke was more than a profession; it was reason for living and breathing. He not only wanted to make poems, he wanted to make the best poems, and he worked at his art with utter diligence. Seager mentions the notebooks filled with sketch-writing-drafts, observations, notes, try-outs. Every afternoon outside his Washington house, Roethke sat with a notebook on his lap, trying out lines and phrases, sentences, prose notes about poetry, *generating language*—everything toward the goal of great poetry. Seager loves to speak of Roethke's notebooks, for *The Glass House* is a book that takes pleasure in the life of writing. Seager is continually intrigued by the creative process, although psychology was not one of his obsessions. Doggedly he explores the relationship between Roethke's mental illness and his genius. I find his speculations suggestive and relevant still on a subject under continual debate: bipolarity and literary achievement.

If *The Glass House* is not the ultimate exploration of Roethke's mind or soul, it is appropriate to notice: For Theodore Roethke, his mind and soul existed to provide material for poetry, like Yeats's voices, which spoke not to discover truth but to provide metaphors for poetry. Even if we disapprove of Roethke's devotion to art, his aestheticism, we must acknowledge that Roethke did not work at language in order to express himself; neither did he devote himself to Blake, Smart, Davies, and Yeats in order to promulgate doctrines or inculcate philosophies. Willy-nilly, his material was his own experience (which included his reading; which included a greenhouse and a father; which included madness) and the ideas or notions he had arrived at—but: *He wrote not in order to embody ideas; he wrote to make poems.* Out of love for the poetic art, he wrote to make objects of that art.

For Allan it was not poems; it was stories and sentences— maybe sentences more than stories. Although *The Glass House* is full of good writing, Allan was dying as he finished the book. If there are lapses, never mind: *The Glass House* is an exemplary biography accomplished under difficult conditions. Allan was limited in quoting from Roethke's poems, a difficulty for a poet's biographer, yet *The Glass House* not only survives this limitation, it profits from it. A descriptive writer's prose becomes better when he understands that his essay will not be illustrated. Seager relies on his own writing, not his subject's. Some of the handsomest language here describes natural history and establishes historical background, as Allan looks to the traditions of Parkman and de Toqueville. In his narrative summary of Roethke's life, Seager finds a tone which is affectionate yet ironic where irony is appropriate. Compare his style to the language of the biographers of Roethke's contemporaries: bad or devious prose deployed to indicate that the biographer is superior to the subject.

Over my years at Michigan I visited Allan often at his big solid gloomy house on Michigan Avenue in Tecumseh—the Michigan house of a Michigan man. Allan derived from the small town of Adrian, not far from Tecumseh; he returned nearly to his place of starting, but in the meantime: At the University of Michigan he was a champion swimmer, and a Rhodes Scholarship took him to Oriel College of Oxford University. After some editing in New York he took to teaching (he taught part-time) while he worked at his fiction. He married Barbara and fathered two daughters, but then Barbara was crippled by multiple sclerosis, which finally took her life in 1966. After Barbara's death, and shortly before his own, he married a second time, his wife Joan. His last years were given over to *The Glass House,* for which he received a Guggenheim. This final work was his elegy for the friend he admired and his eulogy for the life of writing. The last time I saw Allan, at the hospital in Tecumseh with tubes up his nostrils, he had just proofread *The Glass House.*

As it happened, I last saw Theodore Roethke not long before he died. I read my poems at the University of Washington in April of 1963—a decade after the manic invitation—and Roethke died suddenly in July of the same year. When I began my reading, Roethke wasn't there—as I noted without pleasure. I had not seen him since San Francisco State. Frequently he sent me offprints with scrawled little notes, as he sent offprints to many admirers and critics under the impression that he was managing his career. Because his self-promotion was obvious, it was not shrewd—Robert Lowell was shrewder, with his strategic postcards—and I think no one took offense. Once he suggested to his publisher, in so many words, that they put the fix in for the Nobel. Robert Frost—of all people—once complained to me that Roethke was too competitive. If Frost, Roethke, and Lowell (not to mention Yeats, not to mention Pope) were all operators, it seems that operating, albeit unattractive, suggests no inferior ability.

As I read my third poem—Seattle, 1963—Theodore Roethke bulked into the auditorium with his handsome wife, Beatrice. When I finished reading a poem, Roethke would make a noise. Sometimes the noises sounded derisory, sometimes admiring; of course they were disconcerting but they were also funny. When I read a tiny poem about a Henry Moore sculpture, I heard Roethke's gangster-accent curl out of the corner of his mouth: "Read that one again. Read it slower this time." I did; and at a hundred poetry readings since, I have read the poem, told the story, and read the poem over again as "The Theodore Roethke Memorial Re-reading." All in all, it was a crazy afternoon. When I was done Roethke came up to the podium, and David Wagoner showed us the graffito chalked on the classroom blackboard: "The teach blows horses." Then we separated to go to the reception at George Bluestone's house. Roethke and I arrived early, and he led me by the arm to a corner where he sat me down. He sank his great hands into the pockets of his suitcoat and pulled out sheets of galley proof, which he slapped together and pushed at me. "I got a new book coming out," he said. "Read it. It's going to drive Wilbur and Lowell into the *shadows*."

The Far Field is my favorite Roethke, even if it didn't drive Wilbur and Lowell into the shadows. I sat in a corner reading galleys until the party's noises took me over. Roethke was lively and funny, wholly charming—while Beatrice sat unsmiling, looking grim. What a *prude*, I thought, not understanding that Beatrice was grim because she saw mania coming on. Only manics or drunks growl to interrupt poetry readings.

Sitting in the corner, holding the long galley sheets, I read "The Rose" for the first time. A little later, I read it again when it appeared posthumously in the *New Yorker*. A month or two later still, at the American Embassy in London, I read it aloud during a memorial service for four American poets just dead: Cummings, Williams, Roethke, and Frost. I read:

Near this rose, in this grove of sun-parched, wind-warped
    madronas,
Among the half-dead trees, I came upon the true ease of
    myself,
As if another man appeared out of the depths of my being,
And I stood outside myself
Beyond becoming and perishing,
A something wholly other,
As if I swayed out on the wildest wave alive,
And yet was still.
And I rejoiced in being what I was:
In the lilac change, the white reptilian calm,
In the bird beyond the bough, the single one
With all the air to greet him as he flies,
The dolphin rising from the darkening waves;

And in this rose, this rose in the sea-wind,
Rooted in stone, keeping the whole of light,
Gathering to itself sound and silence—
Mine and the Sea-wind's.

This rose grew in the glass house.

Snodgrass's Seasoned Wood

W. D. Snodgrass won the Pulitzer Prize for *Heart's Needle* in 1960. Perhaps, in the memorable language of Richard Nixon, he peaked too soon. When he brought out his second collection, *After Experience* (1968), although it was a better book it received less attention. *The Fuhrer Bunker* of 1977 was sometimes denounced by strategies of misreading. Ten years ago it was commonplace, in summary accounts of contemporary verse, to blame Snodgrass for the abuses of confessional poetry. Thus are the sins of the third generation visited upon the progenitors. One must admit that *Heart's Needle*, with its miseries of divorce and child-loss, started things: Robert Lowell credited his Iowa pupil Snodgrass with showing him the way to *Life Studies*.

Perhaps Snodgrass's *Selected Poems 1957–1987*, beautifully produced by Soho, will find this paleo-conservative new readers among the young, as younger poets look to rhyme and meter again, for Snodgrass is a master of prosody. His meters are enthralling, mad, and multiple, counting whatever can be counted. Within these meters, and without them when he tries a poem free of number, his rhythms are resolute and expressive. He begins with the noise of the 1950s, "Stone lips to the unspoken cave," but continues to explore the thousand things available to formal genius, like this stanza that ends "Lobsters in the Window":

The first half of this essay (now slightly revised) reviewed *Selected Poems 1957–1987* in the *Partisan Review* (1988); the whole appeared in *The Poetry of W. D. Snodgrass* in 1993.

I should wave back, I guess.
But still in his permanent clench
He's fallen back with the mass
Heaped in their common trench
Who stir, but do not look out
Through the rainstreaming glass,
Hear what the newsboys shout,
Or see the raincoats pass.

This poem, from *After Experience,* I would submit to any skeptical eye; the title poem is another.

Snodgrass is one of nature's rhymers. No one in this century has used rhyme so structurally or so semantically or with more serious wit. From the beginning he made rhyme on the off-stress, demanding distortion for meter's necessity: "The hills, the little houses, the costumes" rhymes with "A tourist whispering through the priceless rooms." He rhymes vowels, consonants, dissyllables; he rhymes impossible words with his ear's exactness. Does rhyme lead him to song or song to rhyme? Elizabethan song is audible in early poems, Provençal in later; one remembers that Snodgrass has spent years making rhymed translations (of songs) according to impossible original schemes.

At the start, his poetry recounts personal loss and betrayal. Loss and betrayal continue but turn general as Snodgrass perceives human error (selfishness, treachery, deception, narcissism, murder) first in himself and then in everybody. Appropriately the personal situates itself in the historical; so does the historical. Behind the intimate *Heart's Needle* is Korea; behind the objective or historical *Fuhrer Bunker* is Vietnam. His vision of humanity, bleaker than Calvin's, accounts for some nervous rejections of his work. His poems are hard to take.

Hardest is *The Fuhrer Bunker,* in which Hitler himself, Eva Braun, Goebbels, Goering, Himmler and the rest of the cast speak poetic monologues during the last days of the Reich. This poetry of outrage continually reaches past shock to obscenity, making a catalogue of sin like Dante's Hell without a Purgatory much less a Paradise. The fundamental vision, constantly misread, damns not merely *them*—the Germans or Nazis *out there*—but the viciousness we share with them. In no way does Snodgrass let these people off his hook: we find it offensive that we feel the same hook caught in our own jaw. His protagonists defend themselves, of course, consciously by evasion and rationalizing, unconsciously by splitting attention. Indentations in some monologues present minds wandering distractedly among topics and obsessions, most powerfully Eva Braun's soliloquy when she keeps hearing "Tea for Two." Then there is Hitler's monologue, which zigs and zags from a description of coprophagy to immediate perceptions to plans for suicide and to a sentimental memory of "the cake my mother made." (!)

Form buys speech back. Against expressive evil Snodgrass builds tight grids of shape; the grid itself turns expressive— reflexive, ironic—when Himmler fits his self-justificatory blather onto graph paper. Magda Goebbels poisons her children in ninety-six lines of rhymed stanzas mimicking children's verse. The conflict form engenders is itself obscene, obscenity doubling obscenity with fierce energy to construct a murderous cradle song:

> This is the needle that we give
> Soldiers and children when they live
> Near the front in primitive
>   Conditions or real dangers;
> This is the spoon we use to feed
> Men trapped in trouble or in need,
> When weakness or bad luck might lead
>   Them to the hands of strangers.
>
> This is the room where you can sleep
> Your sleep out, curled up under deep
> Layers of covering that will keep
>   You safe till all harm's past.
> This is the bed where you can rest
> In perfect silence, undistressed
> By noise or nightmares, as my breast
>   Once held you soft but fast.

Long overdue, the *Selected Poems* (overselected; too little from *Heart's Needle*) gathers work out of print, poems printed in small editions, poems never before collected. The final section comes as a relief, more grid and song than pain—though injustice and suffering remain the song's burden. Finally Snodgrass's poems exemplify and affirm endurance despite the horror of things. In some later poems the poet praises birds that keep on singing and trees that live on, seasoned wood and the people who season it.

Thus (with a few changes) I reviewed W. D. Snodgrass's *Selected Poems* for *Partisan Review* in 1988. In the meantime I kept an eye open for other reviews. In the *New York Times Book Review* Snodgrass had some luck. The reviewer was an English poet named Gavin Ewart, able to recognize skill when it clobbered him on the head. In mockery of facts and lists—but in real admiration—Ewart called Snodgrass one of the six best living poets. Because Americans cannot tell when an Englishman is joking, his publishers could advertise that the *New York Times Book Review* called Snodgrass "one of the six best living poets."

In the *Hudson Review* Robert McDowell came to Snodgrass afresh, as if for the first time, dazzled by what he found. This man, he said, is better than Lowell! Wayne Koestenbaum wrote a good review for the *Village Voice,* Bruce Bawer in *Book World;* otherwise, I've not seen the reviews I hoped for: reparations corrective of a rotten consensus. In 1988 reviewing is the scandal of poetry in America. Or maybe *judgment* is. The 1987 prizes came and went with no attention to Snodgrass. "We gave him the Pulitzer in 1960; what more does he want?" I know what I want: critical recognition of priority and excellence.

In 1954 I took a fellowship in writing at Stanford University, one free year with no academic work, no grades or diplomas, time for writing. In a small way I devoted the time to editing as well, for halfway through 1953 I had become poetry editor of the *Paris Review;* in early issues I printed Geoffrey Hill,

Robert Bly, and Thom Gunn. I tried to remain alert for new poets, especially (after two years away in England) the best Americans of my own generation. Eventually I wrote letters to strangers whom I admired as I read them: W. D. Snodgrass, James Wright, W. S. Merwin, Louis Simpson. They sent poems; some became friends.

First was W. D. Snodgrass. Toward the end of my fellowship year I read manuscripts submitted by poets applying for the grant a year hence. Here I found W. D. Snodgrass, whose poems took all my attention, early things later printed in *Heart's Needle*. The marriage of form and energy enraptured me. It was a time in American poetry when form meant rhymed iambic and everybody could do it. Merely scanning and rhyming, after all, is no harder than riding a bicycle—and no more artistic. For seven years I had admired Lowell's driving couplets from *Lord Weary* and lost my breath to Wilbur's gymnastics of stanza; more recently I had appreciated the elegant but thinner performances of young Merrill and Hecht. In 1954 Snodgrass's skill put him quickly into the category of these poets—but he was no imitator and he went places that they couldn't or didn't choose to go. He was darker than anyone except Lowell, even before he found (in the lyrics of "Heart's Needle") the tone or subject area that revolutionized contemporary poetry—and that allowed his teacher the major swerve of *Life Studies*.

Let me look at *Life Studies* and *Heart's Needle* from the other side, from the vantage of the 1940s not the 1980s. The confessional *frisson* was to hear poets revealing conventionally discreditable or politely unmentionable things about themselves. I read at the Mandrake Bookstore in Cambridge (memory claims) an issue of *Partisan Review* with lines from our poet of classical allusion: "Tamed by *Miltown*, we lie on mother's bed . . ." Nobody younger can imagine the shock. This poetry was personal in a way that did not resemble John Donne, Hart Crane, T. S. Eliot, Emily Dickinson, or John Keats. Wordsworth and Whitman had frequently confessed—to virtue, sensitivity, and imagination. In *Heart's Needle* the personal was intimate, miserable, and uncomplacent. In later years, confessional poetry too often turned into a narcissistic whine, into scab-scratching, into the complaint that the world was not more indulgent. Such products find customers: Clearly, we enjoy hearing complaint; especially we enjoy disapproving of the brutes, rapists, and Fascists whom we darkly connect to our parents. Even in good confessional work, readers may entertain complacency—because the violence, hatred, and self-hatred happens outside them in another recognizably neurotic person. We watch, as she told us, the Sylvia Plath Show.

When Snodgrass complains, it is not over accidental circumstances but over the corruption of the human heart, including his own. Nor is this lament the whole of it. Snodgrass brings together the serious fury of extreme states (whether the subject be ostensibly personal as in *Heart's Needle* or ostensibly historical as in *The Fuhrer Bunker*) with the grid or staff that Wilbur plays his tunes on. Surely no one among our poets, not Lowell nor Plath nor Wilbur nor Ginsberg, so combines the sonnet and the scream.

Snodgrass was not offered the scholarship. I asked permission to write him, to ask for poems for the *Paris Review*. Not long ago I found the letter he wrote in answer, the beginning of a conversation which has continued for thirty-five years. Long letters in red ballpoint pen came from Iowa, then from Cornell. It was years before we met. Then as it happened we took jobs near each other, De at Wayne State in Detroit and I at the University of Michigan in Ann Arbor. We picnicked, we played tennis, we met at parties; I went into Detroit, De visited Ann Arbor. During these years we talked poetry but never read each other's manuscript poems.

Then our private lives turned crazy. Remarried De moved to Syracuse, and for several years my children and I stopped with him each summer, at his house in the country, spending a night en route from Michigan to New Hampshire. We ate great meals and stayed up late talking. These were years when De worked with diligence at his apprenticeships to music and to wood, concentrating (as I suppose) on grids that held the precarious world together. I recognized his brave diligence and it served me as model. When I remarried the four of us met each summer in Stratford, Ontario, to watch plays and picnic together. This time was a peaceful interlude for De, like Europe in the summer of 1914.

After I quit teaching and returned to New Hampshire, De went through another divorce and displacement; and our friendship entered another moment. In recent years we have seen each other less frequently—mostly when someone asks us to read together: Bridgeport, New York, Philadelphia, Washington, Norfolk—but our correspondence has flourished. Friendship between writers is the history of literature; so much of it—appropriately enough—is friendship enacted by words on paper. We send each other poems as we work on them—and we work over each other's poems. It gets harder, as you get older, to receive from others the necessary close readings, both negative and encouraging. Old friends die off, get cranky, or become too egotistical. Some younger poets help a lot—but many either love us (which makes them useless) or hate us (which makes them worse than useless). De's work on my poems is invaluable because of his literal mind. His intimacy with what words say, with *all* the baggage they carry whether they acknowledge the load or not, provides him a Johnsonian scalpel. When his thick envelope arrives I sigh deeply, knowing that I will find inside my work's just and courteous ruin. Then I open it.

Flying Revision's Flag

Have you always revised your poems, from the beginning?

At twelve, when I wrote my first few poems, I don't believe I revised. When I was fourteen I got serious and wrote long poems in free verse called "Cain," "Blood," and "The Night Wanderer." Coming home from high school, I shut the door of my bedroom and sat at my desk, working at poems every afternoon for two hours. It astonishes me that, when I finished one of these poems, I turned back to the first page and immediately started rewriting it. It must've been temperament: no one praised revision to me; I don't recall reading about revision in biographies.

Do you recall any teachers or peers who first talked about the revision process?

No. I remember that some teachers were impressed that I revised, but I don't remember anyone urging me to revise. Late in my teens, I discovered Yeats, who of course revised assiduously, not only in drafts before publication but *after* publication, from printing to printing. When I was at college, my senior thesis took account of Yeats's revisions of "The Rose" over more than fifty years. I've wondered since: Do I revise so much because I think that I may therefore grow up to become William Butler Yeats?

An interview with Martin Lammon, published in *Kestrel* in 1993.

Has your inclination to revise diminished or increased over the years?

As I grow older I revise more. It would be nice to think I revise more because my standards have raised themselves, but on the contrary I think it's a Wordsworthian diminishment of inspiration. I *need* to revise more. (Geoffrey Hill said that as you get older the inspiration comes at the end not at the beginning.) I don't mean to say that the quantity of revisions has proceeded evenly. In a depressed period from about 1968 to 1974 I wrote many many drafts but never got much done. Then the "Kicking the Leaves" breakthrough happened— and poems for a while came more quickly, with fewer drafts— I mean maybe twenty-five or thirty drafts over three to five months, as opposed to ninety or a hundred drafts over two years.

When a breakthrough comes, it always seems to me to happen in terms of the sound the poems make. Finding the long line of "Kicking the Leaves"—where I depended less on enjambment than I had done, more on caesuras within the line; where I depended less on vowels and assonance, more on consonants, a line that derived ultimately from Whitman and poets following Whitman like Lawrence, Roethke, Kinnell—I found the line itself an instrument of search or research, exposing for the first time areas of experience and feeling that had always been there but unavailable. Mind you, I married Jane about a year and a half before this breakthrough, and I do not mean to tell you that the private life does not affect the life of art. A year and a half later we moved to the farm. "Kicking the Leaves" *looked forward* to the New Hampshire move—and validated it—in advance.

Could you describe a typical revision process you follow? Or different procedures you follow for different kinds of poems? Has that process—or have these procedures—changed over the years?

When I was twenty-five a poem took six months or a year; typically, now, it takes two years to five. At one time under conditions of extreme inspiration I might write a first draft in which half the final lines were already there; then it took a year or two for the rest of the lines to right themselves. But most likely—and certainly now—the first draft will be terrible, and the second draft considerably different from the first. By the tenth or twelfth draft, things slow down. With a longer poem, I tend to work through several separate fits of working. After a year or so, I get the poem to a point at which I don't know what to do next—but I know it isn't right. I abandon it in disgust for another six months or a year, then come back to it. When I do, the *next* draft changes many, many things—almost like the leap between the first and the second draft: I cut, I rearrange the order of stanzas, I find one line elaborating itself into two new stanzas, a direction I had missed earlier . . . Then the poem gradually settles down again. I may abandon the poem two or three times—and pick it up again—before I get the poem right. If I get it right.

In Their Ancient Glittering Eyes, *you recall how Dylan Thomas claimed to work through a poem by writing two lines a day, finishing each line before moving on toward the completed poem. Have you ever worked that way?*

I couldn't work Dylan's way if you paid me. I lack that concentration; I lack the ability to judge my work without hundreds of nights of sleeping on it . . . Dylan Thomas and Richard Wilbur (and a few others) *know* when they have a line right; I don't.

How do you decide when to stop revising? Can one revise too much?

Difficult question. Galway Kinnell believes that one can revise too much; I'm not certain that *I* can. Sometimes I worry that I may change a word simply because, having stared at it for five years, I'm bored with it. Sometimes I fear that I keep the poems at home because I don't want them to grow up and go away to school. Mostly I think I do the right thing by keeping them around, tinkering and tinkering.

To try drawing a reasonable template: At first the poem is volatile and changeable in the extreme; from time to time it slows down and stops. When it stops and *will* not move again, I show it to Jane and to other friends, and either they tell me to leave it alone, or they show me errors, which I change, or they make demands upon the poem that seem irrelevant to its identity. I finish the poem, with the help of my friends, publish it, it comes out in a magazine—and when the magazine arrives in the mail I tinker with the poem some more.

What do you want to accomplish when you revise? Obviously, you hope to improve the poem, to discover its ideal shape or expression. Would you describe specific goals?

I guess I can't describe goals other than the ones you mention. I'm not discovering "its ideal shape" exactly. I used to think that the statue was there inside the stone and I needed only carve down to it. Now I understand that new things come into the poem during revision, for instance things that have happened *after* I started the poem. Maybe I begin the poem mentioning "death" and then somebody in particular dies; the poem is apparently "about" something that happened after the poem began. Poems are ongoing improvisations toward goals we identify when we arrive at them.

Some writers hesitate to revise older work. When you revise an old poem, what is the relationship for you between the writer you were, say, twenty years ago, and the writer you are now?

I am the irritable elder correcting the young man's mistakes, glad the young man is not around to bite my head off. When I revise an old poem, I'm removing error; I'm substituting not new invention but something that will *do:* invisible mending.

Were you acting as the "irritable elder" or the young man biting off the even younger man's head when you revised your poem "Exile" for The Alligator Bride: New and Selected Poems *(1969)? You have said before that you felt compelled to include this serious one-hundred-line poem from your first book, but that you no longer liked it, so you reprinted as a sort of joke a six-line version comprising three parenthetical couplets from the original, longer version.*

As I get older, maybe I get less irritable. In 1969, "Exile" felt intolerably public, intolerably a platform piece. But I *liked* those parenthetical couplets, ten syllable lines rhyming with six syllable lines; I decided merely to print these six lines as if they were the whole poem; it was only partly a joke. When I did *Old and New Poems* (1990), I felt less touchy about the earlier work. Still, I revised a good many lines of "Exile." It retains its original length of one hundred lines but they're not the same one hundred lines.

Is revision necessary for poetry? Should every poet revise?

Every poet should revise. Revision is not necessary for every poem. It's been necessary for every poem of mine—but I believe the testimony of some poets (and the evidence of manuscripts) that some great poems have arrived spontaneously, or almost spontaneously. Keats seems to have written great poems in a sitting. I find it hard to believe that Allen Ginsberg doesn't revise, as he sometimes claims. I don't *want* to believe it! . . . but it does happen, to other poets.

You may be the most prolific revisionist we have in this country; you've said that one poem has gone through over six hundred drafts over the years. Do you think other poets need to revise their work more than they do? Does the younger poet need to revise more than an older poet?

Six hundred is true enough but anomalous. Some poems go thirty or so, many go eighty, some go a hundred and twenty-five. Maybe Jack Gilbert revises more than I do, maybe Don Justice or De Snodgrass.

Most poets don't revise enough. Most poems that I see—in the mail and in print—have not been gone over thoroughly enough, and include dead metaphors and redundancies and other errors that ought to expose themselves to the inquiring or depressive intellect. I've said it before: You should stare at a poem long enough so that you have one hundred reasons for using every comma, one hundred reasons for every line-break, one hundred reasons for every *and* and *or*. Reasons include rhythm, the emphasis that rhythm bestows, consonants and vowels, and the mouth-joy or dance-movement that *enforces* a line or activates the metaphorical workings of the brain. Reasons can be visual, how the poem looks on the page; reasons can be semantic or formal or the two together. The point is: Try to be *every bit as conscious* as you can possibly be. And all the time you have to know: As conscious as you are, you cannot know everything. If you are lucky, something good may happen in your poem of which you are not aware.

For a while in the sixties, it was common to claim "first thought, best thought"—which seems to me misleading; no: It seems *untrue*. Spontaneity is celebrated only by the nervous intellect, by the intellect afraid of sterility. Some people revise and don't admit it; conversely, others (like me? possibly!) revise less than they claim. All of us distort our stories of process according to our temperaments.

Oh, one celebrated American poet of our moment has written an essay on revision in which it is revealed that the poet revised some poems as many as five or six times. I get poems in the Monday mail that are dated the previous Friday. Never, never, never show a poem to anybody until you have worked on it in solitude for at least six months.

How can you make yourself revise if you don't want to, if your temperament works against your inclinations to revise? Should the poet force himself to revise?

Sure. If the poet wants to be a poet, the poet must force the poet to revise. If the poet doesn't wish to revise, let the poet abandon poetry and take up stamp-collecting or real estate.

In "Writing as Re-vision," Adrienne Rich suggests that revision has a lot to do with the writer's cultural, political, and aesthetic relationship to her subject—how that subject fits into the context of the writer's life. Is "re-vision" for you influenced by social or political issues as well as technical issues?

I'm seldom aware of social or political issues. When I am, I worry about self-censorship. Mostly, I'm just aware of the *faults* of the old word—or mark of punctuation—as inhibiting vision, preventing clarity, or evading difficult emotional truth.

In the early sixties, Robert Bly described you as a poet who examined, challenged, and celebrated the "middle class." Did you agree with that assessment? The way you talk about revision sounds a little like the "work ethic" traditionally associated with middle-class values.

I hate the phrase "work ethic." First, it's traditionally used by Republicans in order to get workers to produce more without extra pay. Second, it sounds as if the only reason to work were duty. I work because I love to work, because I love what I do. Mind you, it's ethical to write better poems rather than worse ones, so if revision promotes excellence, revision is ethical.

Indeed I come directly out of the middle of the middle class and I represent it as much as I criticize it. Bly was a farmer's son—and the agricultural society is considerably different from the suburban middle class I derive from. Virtually all American poets derive from the middle class. Lots claim that they are working class but this bragging often collapses upon examination.

What has revision meant to you over the years? What in particular have you learned about your work? Yourself?

Everything. I love messing about in the mud of language. By this messing about, I learn that my acknowledged motive or feeling was not exactly what I thought it was; revising, I see it myself more clearly. By seeing into myself—seeing *through* myself—probably I see into other people. If I don't see for other people, then my revising is all in vain.

Whom do you see for? Does revision include any responsibility on your part to the integrity of the person upon whom the poem is based, or only to the integrity of the poem itself?

Only to the integrity of the poem itself, but that integrity serves others. I don't care about the subject of the poem—if there is a human subject—but about the object of the poem, and the object of a poem is its readership. "The poem itself" is all the possibilities of people reading it. This possibility controls revision. The poem must talk to somebody who is entirely *not* myself; this notion underlies much revision, as one moves from the *only* private into the *possibly* public. I get this notion from reading poems. After all, I am "the readership" of all the poems ever written by other people. The poems of people long dead continue speaking to me. We talk to each other through poetry. I listen to John Dryden and Robert Browning every day.

Many writers hesitate to show work-in-progress to others, but as you mentioned earlier, you have solicited many readers—both peers and younger writers—for responses to your work. What role do these readers have in your revision process? The readership that represents the "object of a poem"? Or are these readers outside that objective? Does meaningful revision depend upon considering what others might see that the individual poet might miss?

Yes, the real reader may replace and correct the poet's theoretical *other*. Writers who won't show their work to others are avoiding criticism. It's a terrible mistake; tempting, but a terrible mistake. As you get older, it becomes even more necessary to seek out tough readers, because some people will lie to you—not knowing that they are lying, but lying nonetheless. Until recently I have felt that the old boys I grew up with were the best; but people get sot in their ways . . . Some younger friends give me help, hurling my own standards back in my face—or applying standards I haven't even thought of.

First, I need to work on the poem by myself for a long, long time with no other consciousness intruding upon it, no other voice speaking when I look at the poem. After a year or so, when the poem slows down considerably, when I can see nothing more to do about it—but I suspect that there may be things wrong with it—I show it first to Jane, then to others by mail. Most poetic work happens in the original solitude, as you imagine the other, but finally you need the others who are really there: people who read well, people who read skeptically, people who read with imagination *and* intelligence.

Does the poet have a greater responsibility to revise than the novelist, dramatist, or short story writer? Or is poetry simply more conveniently revised?

You mentioned to me before that Robert Bly speaks of a hierarchy of language, with poetic expression at the top of the hierarchy. Poetic expression requires the greatest attention to words in the reading, and therefore the greatest attention in the writing. Attention in the writing largely happens by revision. First by concentration, then by revision. Maybe I am poor at concentrating and therefore need to multiply the occasions of concentration.

When I write fiction or essays I revise a good bit. Some essays and children's books have gone twenty-five drafts and thirty. But I've been able to write and publish some prose in a mere four drafts. When I hit immediately upon a characteristic tone and rhythm and syntax, then I can tidy up in four drafts. It's never so quick in poetry.

Shelley remarked that the poem one writes will never succeed as well as the poem inside one's head. Is revision a way of starting to draw as closely as possible to the poem inside your head?

Shelley was a philosopher who thought he was a poet. There is no poem inside the head. There is the longing toward a poem, the dark leaning, the inarticulate impetus, the dim luminosity . . . You direct a poem in response to the urgency, to *answer* the urgency, but not to copy an ur-poem that exists in your head. The poem is its own words and not some other thing.

Is revision more of a rational or emotional act? Equal parts both? Could you discuss?

In my own case, I need to apply the intelligence—a quality that I must summon with diligence. Therefore I tend to emphasize the rational, but revision's by no means merely rational. A phrase *feels* wrong, so I cross it out. Other words offer themselves as possible substitutes, as words that might *feel* right. When I use *feel* in these sentences, I think of how a glove or a shoe feels right—but *feeling* is the word I use. The phrase revised in the poem is more accurate to feeling; the first phrase was approximate; the second—or the twenty-seventh—is more difficult, more harsh, and more accurate.

In a recent essay in the American Poetry Review, *Alan Shapiro has suggested that creative writing students should "practice imitation" (in the classical sense: that is, the poet contributes original insight to the imitation) of the old forms addressed by the old masters (for example, Vergil, Dante, Milton, Keats). How does revision change for you when you're working on a poem with formal boundaries? In free verse?*

If I did what Shapiro suggests, I did it inadvertently, inadvertent imitation out of love. Lately I have been consciously imitating Horace and Vergil—a long way from the Latin class, where I was never competent. We can learn by imitating provided our ego-strength is sufficient, so that we remain ourselves. New wine in old bottles makes for explosions, and not just destructive ones.

Revision is no different, metrical poetry or free verse. In either case I must find form. Form is not defined by correctly adjacent louder and softer sounds. Meter is mechanics before it is music—though neo-formalists seem seldom to master these mechanics—but it becomes music as much as free verse does. Yeats's notion—that a poem makes a sound when it is finished like the click of the lid of a perfectly made box—applies to free verse as much as to metrical verse.

Do you ever revise a metrical poem into free verse? A free verse poem into something more formally structured?

Yes, I have moved back and forth in my drafts among iambic, syllabic, and the uncountable structures of free verse. Rodin advised young sculptors, when something was not going well, not merely to keep picking at it—the clay, the plaster—but to "drop it on the floor and see what it looks like then." Putting a free verse poem into syllabic couplets; revising from a pentameter stanza into syllabic lines of alternating nines and tens—such alterations drop the poem on the floor, to see what it looks like then.

There's a lot of talk lately about what can and cannot be taught about how to write. Can revision be taught? What can and cannot be taught about how to revise?

Revision can be demanded if it cannot be taught. What must be taught is the ability to see one's errors—possibly beginning with the notion that one *can* err, and that spontaneity is no virtue. Spontaneity tells lies that deliberate, careful thought can alter into truth. When I was a teacher, I doubtless let my students know they would please me more by revising an old poem than by writing a new one. Revision is a flag I've waved my whole life.

Yes, Virginia

In Remembering Poets, *you often refer to Wordsworth's proclamation that, "We poets in our youth begin in gladness; / But thereof come in the end despondency and madness." Is it really gladness that prompts the young poet to begin writing? Having published poetry for over thirty years, what would you say the relation is between age and poetry?*

I don't think that Wordsworth meant that gladness is the *source* of a young poet's writings; or that youth is always happy. He observed that poets are bipolar, and that poetry begins in mania and ends in depression. He looked around him, and he saw aging poets disappear into bitterness and psychosis. When I look at my old poet-friends, I see much anger and misery. I remember these fellows when they were young, giddy, and optimistic; when they felt inklings that they might turn out to be the geniuses of the age, and rich to boot . . . Now I hear them perpetually grump at their own neglect, and at the corruption of an age that ignores them.

Of course it is The Arrangement that occasions this decline, and The Arrangement applies not only to poets. By and large the end of life is "a bad quarter of an hour" that goes on for years. As for me, I feel much more gladness now than I did at twenty—more between fifty and sixty than between twenty and fifty! To date. *To date.*

An interview with Sarah Malloy and Virginia Heffernan published in the *Virginia Literary Review,* 1989; the interviewers are collapsed into one.

Tell about a party you remember from 1971.

In 1971 the party began on New Year's Day for the Rose Bowl Game and did not pause—except for occasional stupor, incarceration, and catatonia—until New Year's Eve, which had an early curfew that year, because in 1972 the party began at the next day's Rose Bowl Game.

Does a poet have to keep moving?

For the last century, most poets who look good a generation later are those who changed considerably during their lifetimes. Some don't. Neither Ransom nor Wilbur nor Moore nor Frost changed very much. Eliot did, Yeats, Pound, Stevens, Williams, Lowell, Berryman—and most of my own contemporaries.

How has the role of the American poet changed since you were in college? What is the fate of the "national bard"?

Does the American poet have a role? Is it Parkerhouse? Is it in the hay? American poets are more public now. There were virtually no poetry readings when I was in college.

The poet's role is to sit at his desk every morning and make poems until they are perfect.

What should readings mean to a poet?

Public confirmation of private labor. The poem comes out of solitude and silence and turns into gregarious noise. I love writing in the darkness of six A.M., at an old desk, with no sound but the mice in the walls and the mouse-scratches of le Pen. But *always implicit*—in the slash that crosses out the word, or in the scrawl that tries another one—is the conviction that "poem" implies a journey connecting the one to the many.

How does living with another poet affect your work?

I don't know; I love it. It is joyous that poetry-talk should be as casual as drinking coffee. It is also a comfort that we share the ups and downs of working at an art. Watching the other is like looking into a mirror but it is *not* looking into a mirror.

Would you hate to appear vain? What are modesty/vanity to a poet?

I know I appear vain! I suppose it is all right if I know my vanity the moment I perform it. What I hate is when I discover, years or hours afterwards, that I have mounted a campaign (or something) solely out of self-regard or self-promotion (1) without knowing it, and (2) (worse) with the conviction that my motives were noble and disinterested!

Do you regret publishing any poem?

Many. And I know that I might be wrong! *Exiles and Marriages* was my first book in 1955, something like a hundred and thirty pages long. I'm not sure that I care for more than thirty pages of it, and most of these pages I have touched up.

Maybe one poem that I particularly *loathe* will turn out to be the only thing reprinted in an anthology a hundred years from now. Sigh. But if I acknowledge this much, what good does it do me? When I come to reprint, I have to follow what I believe *now*. (What I believe now, I must say, is not unaffected by what other people say. When I revise one of these antique poems, I always try it on other people, preferably people who liked the poem the way it used to be.) Sometimes the things I loathe now are just inept—viciously dead metaphors, for instance; but it is the emotional lies that I hate the most. There is a poem called "The Body Politic" that ends with a terrible lie, "Man lives by love and not by metaphor." *Because* it is a lie, people love that line, and this poem used to be anthologized all the time—until I saw what I had made: a ringing ridiculous march-tune of a lie; now I won't let it be reprinted. I have tried to rewrite it but it is hard to reach the style of 1954.* At best I can do invisible mending.

---

*In 1990 I printed a revision in *Old and New Poems*. By 1991 I doubted the revision.

Is there a psychoanalytic escape from "ambition's despair"?

I've never been analyzed. I was in therapy with a psychoanalyst, and it did not cure me of ambition's despair. (It helped me a lot, but it didn't cure me of that.) Most of the people I know who go through genuine analysis seem a little dour. As far as "ambition's despair" goes, maybe they understand ambition's frivolity, so that they are no longer troubled by it.

Mind you, Henry Moore was neither analyzed nor hopeless—and he was surely one of the most ambitious people I ever knew. When he had finished one of his major endeavors, and he sighed to understand that it was not—again, again—incontrovertibly the greatest work of sculpture ever made, instead of jumping off a high building he took a deep breath and started his next attempt to make the incontrovertibly greatest sculpture in the world. If one could seek a temperament, Moore's would be the temperament to seek.

Notes and Notices

John Logan's Language

John Logan: The Collected Poems comes from Boa Editions, from the loyalty and diligence of A. Poulin, who has done so much for contemporary American poetry. Recently, *Painted Bride Quarterly* issued a "John Logan Issue," with some good photographs, some essays of criticism and reminiscence, some poems for Logan, and a tentative bibliography.

Logan was a warm, talented, gregarious man, and his end was melancholy, strokes and increasing debility, until he was— as we were told—found dead on a sidewalk in San Francisco. Robert Hass, in an affectionate essay of reminiscence and praise, tells us: "To get to the roof of his apartment building on Post Street he must have taken an elevator to the top floor, but he had to negotiate the narrow stairway to the roof by himself, leaning on his cane."

There is much affection in this "John Logan Issue," as there should be, and there is also praise for the poems. Reading straight through *The Collected Poems*, I confirmed for myself that John Logan lost his gift long before he died—not the first poet to outlive himself. A little more than halfway through the volume—after *The Zigzag Walk 1963–1968*, with

---

Most of these pieces appeared among the short notices in the *Harvard Review,* over several years beginning in 1987. I intended to review only the products of small presses but extended myself to report on books issued by David Godine and a couple of university presses. I omit many notices in which my sentences were only pegs to hang quotations from.

twenty years to live—Logan's poetry stops or almost stops; fragments of old beauty shine through, but mostly we read two hundred pages of posthumous language trying to find again the splendor of the poet who began. Did the booze do it? Maybe this failure smells of the juniper berry; but other poets have soured as badly, without chemicals to blame. "We poets in our youth . . ."

That unpleasantness acknowledged: How wonderful the best of John Logan is. Surely he is now overlooked, and surely one day he will come back. Maybe this *Boa* volume will do it; or maybe his eager ghost will need to wait another twenty years, for another swing of the pendulum. Logan began in 1955 with the sustained lyrical and ecstatic vision, the resonant language of *Cycle for Mother Cabrini*. His best book is his next one, *Ghosts of the Heart* (1960), in which Logan's ear discovers a quiet, detailed, patient pace, notable in syllabic narratives like "The Picnic," which ends

> And Ruth played with shells she found in the creek,
> As I watched. Her small wrist which was so sweet
> To me turned by her breast and the shells dropped
> Green, white, blue, easily into her lap,
> Passing light through themselves. She gave the pale
> Shells to me, and got up and touched her hips
> With her light hands, and we walked down slowly
> To play the school games with the others.

"A Trip to Four or Five Towns" concludes the book, an ebullient poem of a curious, compelling rhythm. What makes it so strong? It is strong and it is also friendly and amusing. Sometimes Logan uses rhythm as if to mock himself, doing a McGonagall, but the result charms us and fixes his words together.

> And when we visited a poet father
> we rode to Jersey on a motor scooter.
> My tie and tweeds looped in the winds.
> I choked in the wake
> of the Holland Pipe, and cops,
> under glass like carps, eyed us.

That old father was so mellow and generous—
easy to pain,
white, open and at peace, and of good taste,
like his Rutherford house.
And he read, very loud and regal,
sixteen new poems based on paintings by Breughel!

Spring of the Thief (Poems 1960–1962) includes poems written
after Aaron Siskind photographs, as well as a return to
Mother Cabrini. But the title poem is the best, and it ends:

The cords of elm, of cedar oak and pine
will pile again in fall.
The ribs and pockets of the barns will swell.
Winds and fires in the field rage
and again burn out each
of the ancient roots.
Again at last the late November snow
will fill those fields, change this hill,
throw these figures in relief
and raining on them
will transform
the bronze Christ's brow and cheek,
the white face and thigh of the thief.

Logan's finest poems, sturdy and spirited and charming, be-
long to our literature.

Harry Matthews's Poems

Best (if not enough) known for his novels—*Tlooth, The Sinking
of the Odradek Stadium,* and *Cigarettes*—Harry Matthews is also a
poet, sometimes in lines and sometimes in prose. He is a *most*
inventive American writer. In *Armenian Papers* (his *Poems 1954–
1984,* which Princeton published in 1987) there is an extraordi-
nary series of improvisations around an air of Dowland's
("Trial Impressions") as well as the prose-poem sequence of the
title. An editor of *Locus Solus,* a member of OuLiPo, he has
resided largely in France. Dalkey Archive Press issued *20 Lines*

a Day in 1988, paragraphs of daily warm-up (we are told) that do everything and do it well. Matthews makes intricate marks on the surface of his material. Where will the words go next? Why did they go *there* and why is it satisfying that they did?

In 1989 Burning Deck, resolute experimentalists of Rhode Island, collected a new sequence of lined poems in *Out of Bounds*. Reading this series of twenty six-line stanzas, I do not catch—what might not be there; what is probably there—the grid, formal or maybe referential, by which the language assembles itself, but the language (as every time with Harry Matthews) makes intimate local structures of pleasure.

> The blink of abrupt joy conceals beneath the swerving of my
>   forehead
> Two twinkling springs it sometimes in vehement dejection
>   confusedly bursts.
> Now, however, the fervent, needy heart breaks them open in
>   a sorrowful ejaculation that cannot lie
> (An ejaculation incapable of self-cure by venial remedies like:
>   keeping patience with her perfection)
> From lack of power to endure what moves the heart to joy
>   and beggary:
> A withdrawal, a removal, a taking-back, a jovial parting of
>   that holy goal of my infatuation.

Like Andres Serrano, Matthews is an artist of body fluids, of portable and compendious oceans. Indeed, the early seventeenth century underlies his abstract vocabulary not to say his syntax.

> Just as you soothingly conjure the poison of the snake that
>   inside this being perpetually weaves,
> Your viciously benign eye jostles me with uninterrupted fire,
> While, out of mutual effect, justifiable love opens your mouth
>   and sucks from it, fully
> Voiced, celestially human sweetness that often jibes and picks
>   at me almost sternly
> (And vows not lesser cajolery) whose breath pours forth more
>   fragrance and keener

Than, from sky that harbors a failing sun, Javan winds
blowing through crops of cardamom.

Swerving foreheads vow lesser cajolery, yes.

Robert Creeley's Essays

One volume from California collects almost six hundred dense
pages of Robert Creeley's essays (reviews, introductions, remi-
niscences), largely on poetry. Earlier, California brought out
the monumental *Collected Poems* and the *Collected Prose* (which
oddly enough meant Creeley's novel and short stories). This
university press performs a useful service, for as Robert Hass
puts it, Creeley is a master. No one else has so mastered the
quick-moving enjambed free verse lyric line, developed from
Williams's example and taken elsewhere. Creeley has an ear as
acute as Thomas Hardy's, a similar melancholy—and I sup-
pose a similar multiplicity. May he live so long.

Creeley is a New England poet. He writes of Williams: "De-
spite his insistence on this Mediterranean connection, so to
speak, he was as Puritan as I—or Lawrence, or Thoreau or
the Melville of *Pierre*." Although Henry James is a New Yorker
(not to mention an Irishman) he is another Puritan stylist who
resembles Creeley. Take a sentence from *The Ambassadors*,
space it in two-word lines—and you have a Creeley poem
worrying out its self-consciousness.

Some essays here, products of Creeley's fabled generosity,
are easy to skip. But at least four hundred of the pages are
worth close attention: reviews and guide notes from the em-
battled or heroic 1950s and 1960s; weird notes on Swinburne
and appropriate observations on Parkman; and Creeley's won-
derful reminiscence, "On the Road: Notes on Artists and Po-
ets, 1950–1965." Always close to painters, Creeley has written
well about painting, including a passage on Ron Kitaj which I
cherish:

> In Kitaj's art there is such a driven amplitude of attention, so
> many articulate layers of information and care. The axes of

possible directions at times seem infinite—as if one might "go anywhere"—and yet the preoccupation seems to me always rooted in the fact of the human: the singular, the communal, the one, the many, in the places of its history, in the presence of our lives.

How do you like that "driven amplitude"? I turn these words around and apply them to Robert Creeley.

Finally, to interest anyone in looking at this book, let me extract a commonplace paragraph of this man's sentences: "That undertaking most useful to writing as an art is, for me, the attempt to *sound* in the nature of the language those particulars of time and place of which one is a given instance . . ." Of Franz Kline: "There are women who will undress only in the dark, and men who will only surprise them there." Sometimes I delight in his luminous obscurity: "An art begins prior to its conclusion—which is why there can be, with great use, an occasion offering that sense of means which conclusions per se deny." (The next sentence says: "It can be put more simply.") Or: "I like the way this poem moves, in its lines, in the way certain words pick up echos of rhyme in others, sometimes very clearly, sometimes only as a shading. I like the syncopation of the rhythms—most evident if you will make a distinct pause (called a *terminal juncture!*) at the end of each line, and will read the words relaxedly yet clearly, one by one." Or: "The simplest way I have found to make clear my own sense of writing in this respect is to use the analogy of driving. The road, as it were, is creating itself momently in one's attention to it, there, visibly, in front of the car."

Michael Longley's Genius

Few people seem to know it: Michael Longley is a superb poet. He lives in Belfast, publishes with Secker in London, and in the United States comes out of the honorable (but not powerful) Wake Forest University Press. Seamus Heaney writes beautiful poems—but his eminence, no fault of his own, obscures the excellence of Michael Longley, Derek Mahon, and others from the north of Ireland. Our poetic star-system permits us lazily to narrow our reading. But we are indolent or shiftless to miss Michael Longley's small, magnificent "The Ice-Cream Man":

> Rum and raisin, vanilla, butter-scotch, walnut, peach:
> You would rhyme off the flavours. That was before
> They murdered the ice-cream man on the Lisburn Road
> And you bought carnations to lay outside his shop.
> I named for you all the wild flowers of the Burren
> I had seen in one day: thyme, valerian, loosestrife,
> Meadowsweet, tway blade, crowfoot, ling, angelica,
> Herb robert, marjoram, cow parsley, sundew, vetch,
> Mountain avens, wood sage, ragged robin, stitchwort,
> Yarrow, lady's bedstraw, bindweed, bog pimpernel.

Gorse Fires (which follows the rich and brilliant *Poems 1963–1983* of 1985) includes versions from Homer, enigmatic lyrics as short as epigrams, and exquisite lamentations like this stanza about a young man killed in Spain in 1937:

> Buried among the roots of that olive tree, you are
> Wood and fruit and the skylight its branches make
> Through which to read as they accumulate for ever
> The poems you go on not writing in the tree's shadow
> As it circles the fallen olives and the olive-stones.

Longley exemplifies and celebrates the quality of song, a quality largely missing among American poets. It's a lame metaphor, I know, comparing music to poetry, but I mean to praise (as in Irish singing) Longley's arrangements of voice to measure and of sentence against line. Look at the falling-rhythm words in the last elegiac stanza, and at the heart-stopping repetition of "olive" in "olive-stones." In *Gorse Fires* such beauty and tenderness of spirited language fill page after page.

Ruth Stone and Relentlessness

Thirty years ago Richard Wilbur told me about Ruth Stone. *In an Iridescent Time* came out in 1959, *Topography* in 1971, *Cheap* in 1975; now (1987) David Godine beautifully produces

Second-Hand Coat, a new-and-selected poems. When Ruth Stone was young, few women published and fewer were noticed. Now young women poets proliferate, to appropriate remark. In the meantime we have neglected Ruth Stone. Her work has become increasingly powerful. As she grows older her poems turn devastating without abandoning the absolute resolution she learned back in the 1950s. In *Second-Hand Coat* the best work is the latest: art mediates pain neither evaded nor paraded; Ruth Stone writes poems as relentless as a Russian's. Frequently she addresses a dead man, loved and resented, as in "Scars":

> Sometimes I am on a train
> going to a strange city,
> and you are outside the window
> explaining your suicide,
> nagging me like a sick child.
> I have no unbroken rest.
> Sometimes I cover you
> with an alphabet
> or the steers bellow your name
> asking the impossible of me.
> The chicory flowers speak for you.
> They stare at the sky
> as though I am invisible.
> Often the distance from
> here to the pond changes.
> Last night a green fire
> came down like a space ship,
> and I remember
> those people in Argentina
> who went inside one
> where it burnt the grass,
> and forgot their measures
> like clabbered milk,
> forgot who they meant to be
> or suspected they might become,
> and later showed the scars
> on their foreheads
> to everyone,
> begging them to believe.

Reading her, we become the person addressed, whom she begs to believe. Such a poem in its extremity remains memorable, trembling at the shadowy clearing's edge. But Ruth Stone does not only work at the extremes. See the quietness of "Drought in the Lower Field" among newer poems; see her as the Milton of cabbages in "Vegetables I" and "II" and "Separate." Sometimes, especially among the new work, she tells stories of other people; see "What Can You Do" or "Procedure."

But at her best, she accepts nothing from the reader but total capitulation. "Winter":

The ten o'clock train to New York,
coaches like loaves of bread powdered with snow.
Steam wheezes between the couplings.
Stripped to plywood, the station's cement standing room
imitates a Russian novel. It is now that I remember you.
Your profile becomes the carved handle of a letter knife.
Your heavy-lidded eyes slip under the seal of my widowhood.
It is another raw winter. Stray cats are suffering.
Starlings crowd the edges of chimneys.
It is a drab misery that urges me to remember you.
I think about the subjugation of women and horses;
brutal exposure; weather that forces, that strips.
In our time we met in ornate stations
arching up with nineteenth-century optimism.
I remember you running beside the train waving good-bye.
I can produce a facsimile of you standing
behind a column of polished oak to surprise me.
Am I going toward you or away from you on this train?
Discarded junk of other minds is strewn beside the tracks:
mounds of rusting wire, grotesque pop art of dead motors,
senile warehouses. The train passes station;
fresh people standing on the platform,
their faces expecting something.
I feel their entire histories ravish me.

When she addresses "you," her obsession ("Every day I dig you up / And wipe off the rime / and look at you.") is almost unbearable. Finally, however, we do more than bear it. Although shattered, we celebrate Ruth Stone's art, by which the most unendurable (if ineluctable) of human feelings becomes shaped and finished by the will to permanent form.

Learning a Language from Etheridge Knight*

Many years ago as we sat in a living room I asked Etheridge Knight to tell me about the word *funky*. It had leaked into white places and I heard people speak it but I didn't know the word intimately enough to use it. When I asked Etheridge it was early in the evening, a good thing, because three hours later Etheridge was heading around the bend toward the second syllable. I can't remember everything he said; he touched on the middle passage, harvesting tobacco, the tenor saxophone, and professional football.

Poets love words and they must know (or learn) how the language embodies the life in its joy and suffering. We know best what we know deepest, what comes from land, family, culture, and race. About the time I met Etheridge I learned that black was another culture, another language, and another spirit. I had not learned it earlier despite a black roommate at college. (Or maybe *because* of a black roommate in college? In the 1940s a Negro at Harvard *demonstrated* assimilation.) Probably beginning with black music, later from Etheridge and from other black poets (Gwendolyn Brooks, Dudley Randall), later still from Dock Ellis with his street friends and baseball colleagues, I observed a nation or a culture, occupying roughly the same space that my culture occupied, that I was alien to and largely ignorant of. If we touch across this space it is only after (and because) we acknowledge separation. Then—acknowledging separation—we can find sameness: I am someone else for whom ideas of ancestry hang in every air.

Then there is the blue music of a poem like "As You Leave Me":

---

*This note comes from an issue of *Painted Bride Quarterly* devoted to Knight's work.

Shiny record albums scattered over
the livingroom floor, reflecting light
from the lamp, sharp reflections that hurt
my eyes as I watch you, squatting among the platters,
the beer foam making mustaches on your lips.

And, too,
the shadows on your cheeks from your long lashes
fascinate me—almost as much as the dimples;
in your cheeks, your arms and your legs.

You
hum along with Mathis—how you love Mathis!
with his burnished hair and quicksilver voice that dances
among the stars and whirls through canyons
like windblown snow, sometimes I think that Mathis
could take you from me if you could be complete
without me. I glance at my watch. it is now time.

You rise,
silently, and to the bedroom and the paint;
on the lips red, on the eyes black,
and I lean in the doorway and smoke, and see you
grow old before my eyes, and smoke. why do you
chatter while you dress? and smile when you grab
your large leather purse? don't you know that when you
leave me I walk to the window and watch you? and light
a reefer as I watch you? and I die as I watch you
disappear in the dark streets
to whistle and to smile at the johns.

Here is cadence in the service of expression; this poem rises
and falls with its pitches, shouts, and whispers, mainly by sink-
ing on the word *you*. Not right away; *you* doesn't sink in the
title, although it rises in volume to *leave,* in pitch to *leave me.*
But in the first stanza, in "my eyes as I watch *you*," the pro-
noun starts its sinking. The second stanza fills itself with gaz-
ing at the beauty that belongs to *you;* it says *your* five times.
The third stanza begins with *You* all by itself, but it's the last
stanza that makes the poem with its sinking *you:* After it be-
gins "*You* rise," look at the right hand edge of this page: "see
you"; "why do *you*"; "when *you* grab"; "when *you*"; "watch *you*?
and light"; "I die as I watch *you*."

We die too, as this cadence repeats *you* insistently and wistfully, falling into a blue wail of devastation. Again and again the poem dies with this fall, at line's end, to try rising again at the start of the next line by pitch and by volume (*You* is low-pitched and blue, which it rhymes with) "*you*/grow," "*you*/chatter," until it rises (I mean falls) to the utter destitution: "*you*/leave me"; "*you*/disappear."

The devastation of this poem is clear in plot summary: He does this; she does that. But this poem is not plot summary: this poem is song made of natural speech, wailing blue by the skill that comes from word and cadence lived with, learned, and loved.

Wendell Berry's Dailyness*

Some poets remain intimate with the dailyness of life: Thomas Hardy, Gary Snyder. Some poets in their poems imply a removed and holy place, not daily at all: Dylan Thomas, John Milton, G. M. Hopkins. Each way can belong to a great poet; and a great poet, sometimes, can have it both ways: George Herbert's poems are holy and separate, *and* stitch themselves from the intimate fabric of every day. I love the dailyness of Wendell Berry, his line and image integrated with breathing, breakfast, and the working—or the unworking—Sabbath, for that matter. Glancing through the *Collected Poems*, where I have scrawled grateful swoop-marks beside many poems, I am struck by how many poems speak small notes-of-the-day. Many exemplify Berry's pervasive Kentucky wit:

> *Throwing Away the Mail*
>
> Nothing is simple,
> not even simplification.
> Thus, throwing away
> the mail, I exchange
> the complexity of duty
> for the simplicity of guilt.

*From an issue of *Field* largely devoted to Berry.

Daily; but note that he begins to define an abstract system, distinctions made not only between duty and guilt but also between complexity and simplicity. There is also his typical exaggeration, by which he exchanges his Japanese kimono (of precise observation) for the costume of a tall tale, description by fantasy:

The First

The first man who whistled
thought he had a wren in his mouth.
He went around all day
with his lips puckered,
afraid to swallow.

Did he notice that "swallow" is another bird? (Sure. Doubtless after he wrote it down.) Then there's the irresistible combination of grief and joy, the idiom of Eden:

A Meeting

In a dream I meet
my dead friend. He has,
I know, gone long and far,
and yet he is the same
for the dead are changeless.
They grow no older.
It is I who have changed,
grown strange to what I was.
Yet I, the changed one,
ask: "How you been?"
He grins and looks at me.
"I been eating peaches
off some mighty fine trees."

The dreamer gains this gift of combination. Or—one more example—there's the ear or mind which remains open for messages from ordinary things.

Falling Asleep

Raindrops on the tin roof.
What do they say?

We have all
Been here before.

If as a poet you wait on language (or vision) to embody the extreme moment . . . Well, if you are Hopkins we are grateful that you waited . . . Most of us would surely miss what the daily-poet remains ready for. He or she remains attentive to hear the day's world sing its songs.

Tom Clark Moving

We judge the great poets by their great work, not by averaging successes and failures; we don't add the "Horatian Ode" to "Last Instructions to a Painter" and divide by two. Yet with contemporaries we often suspect the prolix and blame the productive. Take Tom Clark, who has published seven thousand poems or maybe only seven hundred. Only the best are good—and they are very good. His early work was fantastic; his middle was St. Marks/Bolinas; his last three books were scathing denunciations of contemporary culture: free verse Augustan satire.

But Clark moves rapidly to exhaust any vein of himself: something new happens in *Disordered Ideas;* we find *some* nasty socially moral satiric free verse ("the gross drone / Of the bourgeoisie shouldn't tempt one / to forget that out there on the / Interpersonal frontier Tab A / Meets slot B for purposes of Insert"), but the fine sneers wane into an eerie fleshy quiet: "Silence is a distillate of noise," this same poem begins, which ends: "The glass boat that floats in / A glass pool to the musical / Silence of a glass etude . . . / Is absolutely unheard."

And now Coffee House Press has produced a beautiful selected poems by Tom Clark called *Easter Sunday.* (Minneapolis leads the country in good small presses, as well as in radio stations and theaters; it is second to Cambridge in bookstores.) *Easter Sunday* collects poems from twenty-five years, from the ephemeral to the permanent; and even the ephemeral is spunky, intelligent, and useful. Clark likes to clash vocabularies, mixing popgrunt with Latinate glory. His satire is strong and difficult, Swiftian in its misanthropy. When he makes a poetry of direct emotional experience, the wound for which satire armors itself, he writes "Dispersion and Convergence," where a surreal iconography carries expression:

> Like musical instruments
> Abandoned in a field
> The parts of your feelings
>
> Are starting to know a quiet
> The pure conversion of your
> Life into art seems destined
>
> Never to occur
> You don't mind
> You feel spiritual and alert
>
> As the air must feel
> Turning into sky aloft and blue
> You feel like
>
> You'll never feel like touching anything or anyone
> Again
> And then you do

Intelligence manipulates all the things of Clark's world. Often his imagination plays not with image or pigment but with idiom, the way Creeley substitutes speech rhythms for imagery. For Clark this is especially true of the nastier satire, gnarls of self-destroying word-sludge. But my favorites are poems of the pictorial imagination. Take the title poem, for instance, "Easter Sunday":

> Someone has frozen the many-storeyed houses
> Under this planetarium
> A brilliant silence like a foghorn
>
> A perfect frieze before the complications
> Arrive with dialogue and
> The olives of daily life
>
> This brown Barcelona paper
> Thrown onto the blue stone of the day
> Makes everyone stop leaving

Through the light in a glass of wine you see them
Under the hot sky of the glacier
Placing their bets then boarding the funeral train

Wesley McNair's Voices

Wesley McNair is a New England poet, preserving the speech and character of a region intimately known. Because he is a true poet, his New England is unlimited: Shorty Towers walks off a roof *everywhere;* Dot has trouble extricating herself from a backseat *everywhere.* Whole lives fill small lines, other people real to this poet and therefore real to us. By his art, Wesley McNair gives us the strangeness of the ordinary: old radios of strangeness, towns of strangeness, strangeness imposed by senility, by rage, by thrombosis; and nothing strange, in *The Town of No,* is anything but ordinary. Here's Dot in the backseat, in "Happiness":

Why, Dot asks, stuck in the back
seat of her sister's two-door, her freckled hand
feeling the roof for the right spot
to pull her wide self up onto her left,
the unarthritic, ankle—why
does her sister, coaching outside on her cane,
have to make her laugh so, she flops
back just as she was, though now
looking wistfully out through the restaurant
reflected in her back window, she seems bigger,
and couldn't possibly mean we should go
ahead in without her, she'll be all right, and so
when you finally place the pillow behind her back
and lift her right out into the sunshine,
all four of us are happy, none more
than she, who straightens the blossoms
on her blouse, says how nice it is to get out
once in awhile, and then goes in to eat
with the greatest delicacy (oh
I could never finish all that) and aplomb
the complete roast beef dinner with apple crisp
and ice cream, just a small scoop.

The Town of No from David Godine is McNair's second book; *The Faces of Americans in 1853* won the Devins Award from the University of Missouri Press in 1984. An award for a first book makes McNair sound like dozens of poets—as does a Guggenheim and a couple of NEAs. But McNair grew up in small-town New Hampshire, graduated from high school in Claremont, majored in education at Keene State, and taught high school. Wesley McNair did not do an MFA at Iowa.

The first thing to notice, reading Wesley McNair, is the noise he makes, or the noises. He has a gorgeous ear for the rubbing-together of adjacent words, as well as the distances between them—as in "fat / tails of cord," where the two *t*'s, widened by the line-break, open a hole you can drive a pickup through. But this mouth-sound is less wonderful than his cadence or rhythm, the magnificent speechlike jerky dance of his free verse, with its unexpected and accurate pauses, its enforced New England pitches. Fat Dot indirectly tells us "how nice it is to get out / once in a while," and "with the greatest delicacy (oh / I could never finish . . .)" eats *everything:* the line-break on "oh" is perfection.

This language is our speech observed-preserved in poetry. By speech are McNair's people fixed in the album of McNair's poetry: life's ruins mostly, drunks, victims of strokes or accidents or general decline, people holding on or trying to hold on, like the mother who tells how one daughter "wasn't / over Fool's Hill / yet"— and then in the confusion of her illness reveals a man's name, "not father nor brother." By the faculty of his *attention*—to people, to their talk—McNair's compassion turns itself into art.

Donald Justice's Music

Donald Justice is in his sixties now. *The Sunset Maker* is retrospective of the 1930s in Florida, depression years tenderly recollected, and the wartime decade following: as the poet says, beginning "Manhattan Dawn (1945)," "there is a smoke of memory / That curls about these chimneys." Like many poets Justice has always made art out of memory.

The Sunset Maker is excellent, as we would expect; it is also unusual. Justice collects twenty-five poems, *and* a handsome essay recollecting the piano lessons *d'antan, and* two crafty short stories. Poems and prose talk to each other; lines sing briefly and beautifully what long paragraphs bulk out with detail. The art of music takes center stage, in a literary book—poems after Henry James, Kafka, Rilke—and one musical phrase does double duty in a poem and a story. The memory of music harmonizes with the music of memory.

But the finest music is Donald Justice's, in the cadence of his line; he is master of numbers, metrical (elegant, devious, shrewd) and free; in his liberty he contrives an unpredictable and artful cage. "Psalm and Lament," an elegy for the poet's mother, includes these lines: "And there is only / This long desolation of flower-bordered sidewalks // That runs to the corner, turns, and goes on, / That disappears and goes on // Into the black oblivion of a neighborhood and a world / Without billboards or yesterdays."

Stony John Haines

Winter News appeared in 1966 out of the heroic first decade of the Wesleyan University Press's poetry series. Many people noticed. When, in 1982, John Haines collected *News from the Glacier: Selected Poems, 1960–1980,* it did not receive enough attention. His new collection, elegantly designed and produced by Story Line Press in Oregon, begins its life by winning a Western States Book Award; maybe people will notice again.

Haines writes lines that look on the page like the poem of our moment—visually or superficially common in the number of syllables in the line, in the number of lines in a poem. But Haines differs from others in the care of his language. He writes with a hard instrument on a hard surface: no disposable verses here. For the most part this book assembles sequences, an older man's accrual of experience and vision. In *New Poems,* take these lines from the fifth part of "Rain Country" (separately issued by Mad River Press):

Remembering, fitting names
to a rain-soaked map:
Gold Run, Minton, Tenderfoot,
McCoy. Here Melvin killed
his grizzly, there Wilkins
built his forge. All
that we knew, and everything
but for me forgotten.

If there is someone who doesn't yet know: John Haines home-
steaded for many years in Alaska; I had hoped to review him
without mentioning Alaska. The poem above, for anyone familiar with Haines, draws
familiar water. Better to show his quality of care and scrupu-
losity, his stone-incising, by quoting him on matters we do not
always associate with his name. Here's the first part of "Days
of Edward Hopper."

These are the houses that stand,
broken and entered; these
are the walls written by rain,
the sparrow arches, the linear
stain of all that will one day
turn to smoke in the mind.

Brick dust was their pigment,
mortar and the grit of brownstone
ground underfoot, plaster
flaked to the purity of snow.

And out of these we entered
the glass arrangements of wind,
became the history of sunlit,
transient rooms, domestic shades;
a substance volatile, so thin
the light of stations burning
at the roadside consumed us. . . .

And out of that the stillness.

Note, please, how beautifully Haines paces his sentences over
the line-breaks, varying the speed of the turn—drawing out a
long *these;* flipping quickly past *thin*—and note, above all, the

stony phrasemaking that presents us, durably visible, "the glass arrangements of wind . . ."

Gerald the Burns

Gerald Burns's essays, *A Thing About Language*, make the fifth volume in the Southern Illinois University Press's *Poetic of the New* series. Three of the original four books derived from the Language Poets, and it's fitting that Burns's title comes from the essay, "A Thing About Language for Bernstein" (Charles, co-editor of old *L=A=N=G=U=A=G=E*). Burns begins this essay with his usual headlong assault on the reader; it's always as if we walked in upon an impassioned monologue, half of an argument, with the antagonist as invisible as the antecedents of his allusions.

> Even the dreadful Maritain distinguishes verse covertly logical or rational from verse which, whether for emotional or exploratory reasons, does float free from "development" of the sort taught in French lycees. Bachelard seems to me to have developed the best devices to criticize it. In English we have Davie's syntactical study, and maybe Charles Williams' *Reason and Beauty*. . . .

We begin to understand that Burns takes a critical stance when we read the first sentence of the second paragraph: "The trouble, my trouble, comes from the relation of theory to practice, fiery theory and tepid practice." I like the way his prose revises itself as it moves on the page, the mind caught in the act of thinking. This brief "Thing About Language for Bernstein" ends:

> Max Picard says if words didn't go out of themselves or refresh themselves *in* things, they would hang around in heaps and impede our movements, like things in a warehouse. That *may* be an argument for reference. One could prefer the warehouse, as one dreams in a surplus-parts store. Will this be sought out or printed—ever be more than *browsing*. And is there, built into some kinds of experiment as result, the utility of browsing only. Please reply.

The door closes, the speech concludes—and no one has answered it. In a moment we will walk into another room, to hear another speech by Gerald Burns: passionate, brilliant, and baffling.

Speech it is, *always*. I love the rhythms of these essays, which allude with a runic music like Guy Davenport's, with something like Davenport's scrupulous attention to verbal nuance. Burns eludes affectation by charm. We come to feel: *This is the only way that Gerald Burns can talk.* Is any other writer so much of a piece throughout? Burns's poems are virtually indistinguishable in tone, allusion, diction, and pace from his diaries and his essays. A firm, startling voice speaks—obsessively, obscurely, intelligently. Burns never states; he hints, winks, alludes, conspires. If you can hear the music, you cannot help but dance. In his Introduction, Robert Creeley speaks of Burns as the consummate *reader,* comparing him to Pound. Later Creeley connects Burns to their joint enthusiasm, Edward Dahlberg, whose language (but not whose irascibility) further defines the Burnshood of Burns.

We read Gerald Burns by taking the plunge; by accepting his voice, his agenda, and his difficulty. We emerge battered and revised.

Poets Talking*

The first poets-at-work interview took place in 1619 at Hawthornden in Scotland. Ben Jonson walked north from London, pausing to commission a pair of shoes, and spent some weeks with his friend William Drummond. Drummond took note of Jonson's remarks, apparently without letting his subject know that he was being recorded. When his guest departed, Drummond summed him up: "He is a great lover and praiser of himself, a condemner and scorner of others, given rather to lose a friend than a jest, jealous of every word and action of those about him, especially after drink, which is one

---

*These paragraphs derive from the introduction to *Poets at Work,* interviews from the *Paris Review,* published by Viking in 1989.

of the elements in which he lives . . ." (Drummond, it must be conceded, was another of the *genus irritable vatum.*) In Drummond's transcript Jonson speaks of prosody on occasion, but mostly delivers judgment: Samuel Daniel is a good honest man but no poet; John Harrington's *Ariosto* is the worst translation ever made; Shakespeare wants art . . . In a few of his remarks, he grudges favor; he is even generous. Although he avers that John Donne deserves hanging for getting his meter wrong, elsewhere he allows that Donne is "the first poet in the world, in some things . . ."

Poets like to talk about poetry. In *Paris Review* interviews, poets speak in tones that we recognize as characteristic. When her interviewer asked how old she was on some occasion, Marianne Moore supplied two pieces of information and asked, "Can you deduce my probable age?"

All of these interviews share the manner of a characteristic voice. Here are nine passages from the tabletalk of nine poets:

a) You've got to *score*. They say not, but you've got to score . . .
b) If the stone isn't hard enough to maintain the form, it has to go out.
c) . . . my slight product . . . conspicuously tentative— . . .
d) I wonder what an "intention" means. One wants to get something off one's chest.
e) I am an actress in my own autobiographical play.
f) It's a feeling that begins somewhere in the stomach and rises up forward in the breast and then comes out through the mouth and the ears.
g) Hughes writes the kind of stuff I throw away.
h) There's nothing more embarrassing than being a poet.
i) . . . from the moment life cannot be one continual orgasm, real happiness is impossible.

Match with: (1) Elizabeth Bishop, (2) John Ashbery, (3) Robert Frost, (4) Marianne Moore, (5) Ezra Pound, (6) T. S. Eliot, (7) James Dickey, (8) Anne Sexton, (9) Allen Ginsberg.*

**a/*3; *b/*5; *c/*4; *d/*6; *e/*8; *f/*9; *g/*7; *h/*1; *i/*2.

Poets like to tell stories as much as novelists do. Some poets' dialogue might be best suited to the stage, possibly in a review called *The Poetry Follies.*

Marianne Moore: The theater is the most pleasant, in fact my favorite form of recreation.
Interviewer: Do you go often?
Marianne Moore: No, never.

Frost describes his first meeting with Pound ("He was all silent with eagerness") so that we can set it on the stage, although Frost's jujitsu story ("He grabbed my wrist, tipped over backward, and flipped me over his head") may remain too improbable for theater. Pound himself is never so relaxed as when he eases into anecdote. When the ill William Carlos Williams tires and his wife, Flossie, takes over, she tells how the doctor and his family—the *only* artistic types with a permanent address—give shelter to Bohemian friends over the decades: Marsden Hartly, John Reed . . . Apparently Maxwell Bodenheim faked a broken arm in order to avail himself of the Williams's hospitality. Conrad Aiken tells that story better than Flossie does. One of our pleasures in reading these interviews is to watch the same scenes from differing viewpoints. Eliot, Pound, Aiken, and Frost all touch on poetic London before the Great War. Elizabeth Bishop is another who tells a story well, including an account of a poetry reading by the young Robert Lowell; maybe her interview is best of all.

Many of these interviews are the most-quoted sources when critics write about the life and the work together. Writers constantly cite Eliot above (d) without reference to its source. These interviews are literary history as gossip, full of famous revelations that have become commonplace. Reading them is like discovering that Shakespeare and Pope are composed of book titles. We find not only familiar revelations but also the classic texts for poetic *ideas,* like the Ginsberg interview with its doctrines of spontaneity. That interview especially preserves its historical moment intact, detailed and colorful, like a Pompeii under the ashes of Vesuvius.

These oral histories were almost always revised by reflection, distance, and the ballpoint pen. I remember Eliot finding that the word "creature," applied to Conrad Aiken in cold print, sounded more condescending than he intended to show himself. If something true is lost by revision, I suspect that far more is gained. The moment is finer for a coat of varnish. Gossip becomes archival.

It is true that the phenomenon of these *Paris Review* interviews, begun in 1952, pointed toward the culture of celebrity. When George Plimpton talked with E. M. Forster at Kings College, he did not know that he surveyed the highway for Andy Warhol and *Interview*. From that beginning the interview printed as dialogue has become a common literary form for better and worse but mostly for worse. The *Paris Review* interviews have been consistently better than others—because they follow the tone established almost forty years ago, in which the interviewer remains almost anonymous. The questioner is a version of ourselves; dressed in the costume of the common reader, the questioner forgoes the egotism of a voice; the interviewer is ourself gifted with a key to the *atelier*, gifted maybe with a greedy ear . . .

A recurrent theme in *Poets at Work* is collaboration. This book displays considerable egotism, yet for the most part these egos accept the help of others and proffer their own help in return. There is the famous case of Pound cutting the manuscript of *The Waste Land*—of which Eliot's account here was for long our most revealing source. "[Pound] didn't try to turn you into an imitation of himself." Later Eliot speaks of his profession as an editor who made suggestions on the manuscripts of younger poets for decades. Pound tells us about working with Yeats and Ford. Elsewhere, we hear of Richard Eberhart counseling the young Robert Lowell, the slightly older Lowell sharing himself between Allen Tate and John Crowe Ransom, the moderately still older Lowell going to Randall Jarrell and Stanley Kunitz. Common is the search for help, which is also the search *to* help. We hear of Ginsberg working with William Burroughs and Jack Kerouac, Sexton with Maxine Kumin, Bishop with Frank Bidart, Robert Fitzgerald with Flannery O'Connor.

Of course there is counter motion to community, some of it

comic like Ben Jonson's bitchery. When the interviewer asks James Dickey if he corresponds with other poets, Dickey tells us that he is "almost completely out of touch with them. They often write to me, but because of my heavy schedule I almost never have time to answer." Robert Frost tells stories of London in the teens that reveal his contempt for poets who help each other. When he says of Pound, Flint, Aldington, H.D., and Hulme that "they met every week to rewrite each other's poems," his voice loads itself with deprecation; he told them (as he tells us) that this workshopping "sounded like a parlor game to me," and adds that he was "just kidding." Ho ho. It was life and death to Frost to do his own work, all alone—and to stop there.

Frost was the exception. The history of poetry is a history of rivalries which are also friendships, not only Pound and Williams, Pound and Eliot, Pound and Yeats, not only Dylan Thomas and Vernon Watkins, but Wordsworth, Coleridge, and Southey; Keats and Leigh Hunt, not to mention neoclassicists and Elizabethans in their coffee houses and ginmills. Not to mention the footsore Ben Jonson drinking sack, running down his peers, and distributing morsels of praise.

The community of poets surprises us because we entertain stereotypes associating poets with lonely alienation. Generosity is typically part of the poet's work. This community is not—or it need not be—the sordid business of favor-trading; nor is it merely a series of acts of kindness, like Boy Scouts helping old folks across the streets. It resembles more nearly the DNA that uses human bodies to replicate itself. This collaboration supports a mutual and enduring endeavor. Poets do not take turns helping each other over difficulties: They work together to build the house of poetry.

Young Bly

He didn't seem young at the time. In February of 1948, my freshman year at Harvard, I first met Robert Bly—in the sanctum of the *Harvard Advocate* on Bow Street. He was Bob for twenty years, and he will become Bob again—for my comfort—as I recollect him here. The magazine occupied several rooms on the second floor above the Gold Coast Valeteria, near Adams House and adjacent to the more prosperous *Harvard Lampoon*. I read a notice advertising this term's competition for the *Advocate* and I decided to compete, to try to join a literary board that included Kenneth Koch, John Ashbery, and Robert Bly.

Not that I knew whom I was joining. I was merely terrified, an infant among the grown-ups. Most of the *Advocate*'s editors (as of 1948) were veterans of the war that had ended two and a half years earlier. I came to college straight from boarding school and sat next to people two years older, who had fought in France or Saipan; the ordinary difference of age seemed multiplied by seven. In 1987, Robert Bly and I are the same age, but in February of 1948 Bob seemed as old and as bronze as John Harvard in the Yard. His naval career had taken place in technical schools studying radar, and then in a hospital where he had rheumatic fever—but I didn't know that.

Although it's unlikely, I think I remember our first meeting: He wore a three-piece brown tweed suit and brown shoes with a narrow maroon tie, striped with green, showing above his vest and below the collar of his buttoned white shirt. He was skinny, incredibly skinny, I assumed from excess of intelli-

Originally published in *Grunt*, 1987.

gence; he wore intelligent horn-rimmed glasses; he spoke rarely, opening his mouth narrowly, with compunction and reticence. He never, ever smiled. Probably I thought he was thirty, some extravagant figure of years. We talked poetry right away, about Robert Lowell I believe; Lowell really *was* thirty. We both admired him, and we spoke of an earlier *Advocate* dialogue about *Lord Weary's Castle*. The literary ambience was different in those days, and people argued passionately about Lowell's enjambments; friendships dissolved in disagreement over eccentric caesurae. Bob and I saw eye to eye—with the result that we found each other intelligent. Mind you, if we had acknowledged our judgment, we would not have used the word "intelligent." At Harvard in 1948, people spoke a special language, and "rather bright" was high commendation. For "rather bright" read "extremely intelligent" throughout; for "not very bright" read "incredibly stupid."

At some point soon, Bob Bly and I dropped our guards and became best friends—which we have remained over decades of affection and argument. When I knew him at first, his poems occupied the closet and he was known as a critic; I suspect that poetry was too important, too much heart-work to be taken public at cutthroat Harvard. But it was not long before we were showing each other our poems, revising each other, reading other people's work, and arguing about what we read. I remember vividly the excitement of his young energy, his enthusiasm, and the generosity of his attentions to my work. Maybe twice a week we met to talk, to argue, to rewrite each other. We took no courses together, until two years later when we were both in Archibald MacLeish's first creative writing class, but we handed to each other what we learned elsewhere. John Kelleher was Bob's tutor, and as a result I felt as if I had a half-tutorial with John Kelleher.

At the *Advocate* the editors stayed up half the night arguing over whether a given poem was good enough for our magazine. Doubtless our solemnity derived from self-importance— but the seriousness of our arguments helped us grow up. Not that we were serious on all occasions. We had marvelous parties, especially when poets came to town to read in Harvard's Morris Gray series. Remember that until a decade later, poetry readings were rare in the United States. We distributed gallons of martinis at parties for Eliot, Thomas, and the Sitwells.

It was Bob who discovered Adrienne Rich at a Radcliffe jolly-up, telling me that he had met a girl from Baltimore who knew *all* about modern poetry. He introduced me, and we double-dated at Jim Cronin's, Bob with another girl (beautiful, bright, blonde—and in later life a banker. I met her again in 1990 and asked her, "What did we *do* on those dates?" She told me, "You and Adrienne and Robert said your poems"). One time when he was a senior, Bob and I drove to Bennington for a blind double-date—he owned a vast rusty green Buick—and on the way home Bob screeched to a stop beside a field of alfalfa. He handed me the keys, so that he might remain with the alfalfa; he thumbed back to Harvard later; I drove the car.

In the first summer of our friendship we hitchhiked down south together; or we started to. We spent one night in the woods sleeping on springs in a lean-to we happened upon. Shortly after we settled in, a troop of Boy Scouts arrived, properly outfitted with sleeping bags and cooking equipment. When we exposed our supplies—two cans of Vienna sausage, as I remember—the scoutmaster's mouth dropped open: "Is *that* your *gear?*" The next day Bob stopped a car, claiming that we had been chased by a bear, and we conned ourselves a ride. That night we rented a four-dollar room in a small Tennessee town to get a little sleep, and the next day we argued over who would thumb rides standing in the sun while the other napped in the shade of a stone wall. I headed back north by myself. I thought: I'll never see *him* again!

We overlapped three years at college, writing and arguing and double-dating together. When he won Harvard's Garrison Prize for Poetry in his senior year, he beat me out. We waited together at Warren House for the winner's name to be posted. When his name went up on the wall—Bob remembers—I *immediately* claimed: "I'm not jealous." (I won it the next year, only because the prize was reserved for men; Adrienne Rich was Yale Younger Poet as I won the Garrison.) A year ahead of me,

Bob graduated and went to New York, which made Harvard lonely in my senior year.

He was extraordinary, even then, for his unceasing curiosity—and for his volatility. Both of us kept moving, rocketing among enthusiasms, but he was quicker than I was. He wrote lyrics influenced by Lowell, blank verse monologues less influenced by Lowell, plays, Shakespearean sonnets . . . When I was at Oxford in the winter of 1951–52, he sent me a handful of sonnets, which I started to go over—revising, making notes—until I was interrupted by a letter from New York. I think of that letter as foreshadowing the Robert Bly who emerged so strongly in the 1960s: Don't bother with those sonnets, he wrote me; they're too old-fashioned . . .

Interview with Peter Stitt

I would like to begin by asking how you started. How did you become a writer? What was the first thing that you ever wrote and when?

Everything important always begins from something trivial. When I was about twelve I loved horror movies. I used to go down to New Haven from my suburb and watch films like *Frankenstein, The Wolf Man, The Wolf Man Meets Abbott and Costello.* So the boy next door said, "Well, if you like that stuff, you've got to read Edgar Allan Poe." I had never heard of Edgar Allan Poe, but when I read him I fell in love. I wanted to grow up and *be* Edgar Allan Poe. The first poem that I wrote doesn't really *sound* like Poe, but it's morbid enough. Of course I have friends who say it's the best thing I ever did:

> Have you ever thought
> Of the nearness of death to you?
> It reeks through each corner,
> It shrieks through the night,
> It follows you through the day
> Until that moment when,

This interview, from the *Paris Review* series, repeats topics and anecdotes approached in other interviews and essays. George Plimpton wanted archival coverage, and therefore Peter Stitt (on the stage of the Poetry Center at the uptown Y and elsewhere) asked for stories that remembered poets, available in *Their Ancient Glittering Eyes* (1992). Rather than cut and fragment this interview, I have elected to repeat myself.

In monotones loud,
Death calls your name.
Then, then, comes the end of all.

The end of Hall, maybe. That started me writing poems and stories. For a couple of years I wrote them in a desultory fashion because I wasn't sure whether I wanted to be a great actor or a great poet.

Then when I was fourteen I had a conversation at a Boy Scout meeting with a fellow who seemed ancient to me; he was sixteen. I was bragging and told him that I had written a poem during study hall at high school that day. He asked—I can see him standing there—"You write poems?" and I said, "Yes, do you?" and he said, in the most solemn voice imaginable, "It is my profession." He had just quit high school to devote himself to writing poetry full time! I thought that was the coolest thing I'd ever heard. It was like that scene in *Bonnie and Clyde* where Clyde says, "We rob banks." Poetry *is* like robbing banks. It turned out that my friend knew some eighteen-year-old Yale freshmen, sophisticated about literature, and so at the age of fourteen I hung around Yale students who talked about T. S. Eliot. I saved up my allowance and bought a little blue, cloth-covered collected Eliot for two dollars and fifty cents, and I was off. I decided that I would be a poet for the rest of my life, and started by working at poems for an hour or two every day after school. I never stopped.

What about at your high school? I believe you attended Exeter—was anyone helpful to you?

After a couple of years of public school, I went to Exeter—an insane conglomeration of adolescent males in the wilderness, all of whom claimed to hate poetry. There was support from the faculty—I dedicated *A Roof of Tiger Lilies* to one teacher and his wife, Leonard and Mary Stevens—but of course there was also discouragement. One English teacher made it his announced purpose to rid me of the habit of writing poetry. This was in an English Special, for the brightest students, and he spent a fifty-minute class reading aloud some poetry I'd handed him, making sarcastic comments. For the first ten minutes, the other students laughed—but then they shut up. They may not have liked poetry but they were shocked by what he did. When I came back to Exeter ten years later to read my poems, after publishing my first book, the other teachers asked my old teacher-enemy to introduce me, and my mind filled up with possibilities for revenge. I did nothing, of course, but another ten years after that apparently my unconscious mind did exact its revenge—and because I didn't intend it, I could enjoy revenge without guilt. I wrote an essay for the *New York Times Book Review* that offered a bizarre interpretation of Wordsworth's poem about daffodils. At the end, I said that if anyone felt that my interpretation hurt their enjoyment of the poem, they'd never really admired the poem anyway—but just some picture postcard of Wordsworth's countryside that a teacher handed around in a classroom. When I wrote it, I thought I made the teacher and his classroom up—but a few days after the piece appeared, I received the postcard in an envelope from my enemy-teacher at Exeter together with a note: "I suppose your fingerprints are still on it."

Was there anyone else when you were young who encouraged you to be a writer?

Not really. My parents were willing to let me follow my nose, do what I wanted to do, and they supported my interest by buying the books that I wanted for birthdays and Christmas, almost always poetry books. When I was sixteen years old I published in some little magazines, and my parents paid for me to go to Bread Loaf.

I remember the first time I saw Robert Frost. It was opening night, and Theodore Morrison, the director, was giving an introductory talk. I felt excited and exalted. Nobody was anywhere near me in age; the next youngest contributor was probably in her mid-twenties. As I was sitting there, I looked out the big French windows and saw Frost approaching. He was coming up a hill, and as he walked toward the windows first his head appeared and then his shoulders, as if he were rising out of the ground. Later, I talked with him a couple of times and I heard him read. He ran the poetry workshop in the afternoon on a couple of occasions, though not when my poems were read, thank God; he could be nasty. I sat with him one time on the porch as he talked with two women and me. He delivered his characteristic monologue—witty, sharp, acerbic on the subject of his friends. He wasn't hideously unkind, the way he looks in Thompson's biography, but also he was not Mortimer Snerd; he was not the farmer miraculously gifted with rhyme, the way he seemed if you read about him in *Time* or *Life*. He was a sophisticated fellow, you might say. We played softball. This was in 1945, and Frost was born in 1874, so he was seventy-one years old. He played a vigorous game of softball but he was also something of a spoiled brat. His team had to win, and it was well known that the pitcher should serve Frost a fat pitch. I remember him hitting a double. He fought hard for his team to win, and he was willing to change the rules. He had to win at everything. Including poetry.

What was the last occasion on which you saw him?

The last time I saw him was in Vermont, within seven or eight months of his death. He visited Ann Arbor that spring and invited me to call on him in the summer. We talked about writing, about literature, though of course mostly he monologued. He was deaf, but even when he was younger he tended to make long speeches. Anyway, after we had been talking for hours, my daughter Philippa, who was three years old, asked him if he had a TV. He looked down at her and smiled and said, "You've seen me on TV?"

Also we talked about a man who was writing a book about Frost, another poet I knew. Frost hadn't read his poetry, and he asked me, "Is he any good?" I told him what I thought. Then, as we were driving away, I looked into the rearview mirror and saw the old man, eighty-eight, running after the car—literally running. I stopped and he came up to the window and asked me please, when I saw my friend again, not to mention that Frost had asked me if his poetry was any good, because he didn't want my friend to know that he had not read his poetry. Frost was a political animal in the literary world. So are many of the best poets I run into, and it doesn't seem to hurt their poetry.

Our meeting is an occasion of sorts, since you are the original interviewer of poets for the Paris Review. *Whom did you interview?*

T. S. Eliot, Ezra Pound, and Marianne Moore. I had already known Eliot for a number of years. At the time of the interview, he was returning from a winter vacation in someplace like the Bahamas, and we did the interview in New York. He looked tan and lean and wonderful, which surprised me. I had not seen him then for two or three years, and in the meantime he had married Valerie Fletcher. What a change in the man! When I *first* met him, in 1950, he looked like a corpse. He was pale and bent over; he moved stiffly and slowly and coughed a continual, hacking cough. This ancient character was full of kindness and generosity, but he looked ready for the grave, as he did the next several times I saw him. Then, when I met him for the interview after his second marriage, he looked twenty years younger. He was happy; he giggled; he held hands with his young wife whenever they were together. Oh, he was an entirely different person, lighter and more forthcoming. Pound I interviewed in the spring of 1960. I was apprehensive, driving to see him in Rome, because I was afraid of what I'd run into. I had loved his poetry from early on, but his politics revolted me, as they did everybody. The *Paris Review* had scheduled an interview with him once before, when he was at St. Elizabeths, but he canceled at the last minute because he determined that the *Paris Review* was part of the "pinko usury fringe." That's the sort of thing I expected, but that's not what I found. He was staying with a friend in Rome, and I drove down from England with my family. After I had knocked on the door and he swung it open and made sure it was me, he said, "Mr. Hall, you've come all the way from England—and you find me in fragments!" He spoke with a melody that made him sound like W. C. Fields. There's the famous story—this didn't happen to me but I love it—of a young American poet who was wandering around in

Venice, not long before Pound died, and recognized the house where Pound was living with Olga Rudge. Impulsively, he knocked on the door. Maybe he expected the butler to answer, but the door swung open and it was Ezra Pound. In surprise and confusion the young poet said, "How are you, Mr. Pound?" Pound looked at him and, as he swung the door shut, said, "Senile."

The Pound I interviewed in 1960 had not yet entered the silence, but the silence was beginning to enter him. There were enormous pauses in the middle of his sentences, times when he lost his thread; he would begin to answer, then qualify it, then qualify the qualification, as though he were composing a Henry James sentence. Often he could not find his way back out again, and he would be overcome with despair. He had depended all his life on quickness of wit and sharpness of mind. It was his pride. Now he was talking with me for a *Paris Review* interview, which he took seriously indeed, and he found himself almost incapable. Sometimes after ten minutes of pause, fatigue, and despair, he would heave a sigh, sit up, and continue the sentence where he had broken it off. He was already depressed, the depression which later deepened and opened that chasm of silence. But then and there, in 1960, I had a wonderful time with him. He was mild, soft, affectionate, sane. One time he and I went across the street to have a cup of coffee at a place where I had had coffee earlier. The waiter recognized us both, though he had never before seen us together, and thought he made a connection. He spoke a sentence in Italian that I didn't understand, but the last word was *figlio*. Pound looked at me and looked at the waiter and said, "*Sì*."

In the interview with him, your questions are challenging, yet he seems, not evasive exactly, but as though he just did not quite understand what he had done.

Oh, no, he never really understood. He insisted that there could be no treason without treasonable intent. I'm certain that he had no treasonable intent, but if treason is giving aid and comfort to the enemy in time of war . . . he broadcast from Rome to American troops suggesting that they stop fighting. Of course he thought he was aiding and comforting the real America. He wasn't in touch with contemporary America, not for decades. All the time he was at St. Elizabeths he was in an asylum for the insane, and his visitors were mostly cranks of the right wing. The news he heard was filtered. I think you can chart his political changes right from the end of the First World War and find that they correlate with the growth of paranoia and monomania that connected economics—finally, Jewish bankers—with a plot to control the world. He started out cranky and moved from cranky to crazy.

In Remembering Poets, *just as now, the one poet you interviewed that you don't talk about is Marianne Moore.*

Back then, I thought I didn't have enough to say—or enough that other writers hadn't already said. Lately, I've come up with some notions about her that I may write up for a new edition of that book.* I had lunch with her twice in Brooklyn. The first time she took me up the hill to the little Viennese restaurant where she took everybody. Like everybody else I fought with her for the check and lost. She was tiny and frail and modest, but oh so powerful. I think she must have been a weight lifter in another life—or maybe a middle linebacker. Whenever you're in the presence of extreme modesty or diffidence, *always* look for a great degree of reticent power, or a hugely strong ego. Marianne Moore as editor of the *Dial* was made of steel. To wrestle with her over a check was to be pinned to the mat.

Another time when I came to visit, her teeth were being repaired so she made lunch at her apartment. She thought she looked dreadful and wouldn't go outside the house without a complete set of teeth. Lunch was extraordinary! On a tray she placed three tiny paper cups and a plate. One of the cups contained about two teaspoons of V-8 juice. Another had about eight raisins in it, and the other five and a half Spanish

---

Their Ancient Glittering Eyes: Remembering Poets and More Poets came out in 1992.

peanuts. On the plate was a mound of Fritos, and when she passed them to me she said, "I like Fritos. They're so good for you, you know." She was eating health foods at the time, and I'm quite sure she wasn't being ironic. She entertained some notion that Fritos were a health food. What else did she serve? Half a cupcake for dessert, maybe? She prepared a magnificent small cafeteria for birds.

Marianne Moore went to school and she wrote poetry, but she did not study creative writing in school. Do you think the institution of the creative writing program has helped the cause of poetry?

Well, not really, no. I've said some nasty things about these programs. The Creative Writing Industry invites us to use poetry to achieve other ends—a job, a promotion, a bibliography, money, notoriety. I loathe the trivialization of poetry that happens in creative writing classes. Teachers set exercises to stimulate subject matter: "Write a poem about an imaginary landscape with real people in it." "Write about a place your parents lived in before you were born." We have enough terrible poetry around without encouraging more of it. Workshops make workshop poems. Also, workshops encourage a kind of local competition—being better than the poet who sits next to you—in place of the useful competition of trying to be better than Dante. Also, they encourage a groupishness, an old-boy and -girl network that often endures for decades.

The good thing about workshops is that they provide a place where young poets can gather and argue—the artificial café. We're a big country without a literary capital. Young poets from different isolated areas all over the country can gather with others of their kind.

And I suppose that workshops have contributed to all the attention that poetry's been getting in the last decades. Newspaper people and essayists always whine about how we don't read poetry the way we used to, in the 1920s for example. Bullshit! Just compare the numbers of books of poems sold then and now. Even in the 1950s, a book of poems published by some eminent poet was printed in an edition of one thousand hardback copies. If it sold out everyone was cheerful. In

1923 *Harmonium* didn't sell out—Stevens was remaindered, for heaven's sake! A book of poetry today, by a poet who's been around, will be published in an edition of five to seven thousand copies and often reprinted.

But it's not the Creative Writing Industry itself that sells books; it's the poetry readings. Practically nobody in the twenties and thirties and forties did readings. Vachel Lindsay, early, then Carl Sandburg, then Robert Frost—nobody else. If you look at biographies of Stevens and Williams and Moore, you see that they read their poems once every two years if they were lucky. Poetry readings started to grow when Dylan Thomas came over in the late 1940s and 1950s. By this time there are three million poetry readings a year in the United States. Oh, no one knows how many there are. Sometimes I think *I* do three million a year.

In the 1960s, when the poetry reading boom got going, people went to their state universities and heard poets read. When they went back to their towns, they got the community college to bring poets in, or they set up their own series through an arts group. Readings have proliferated enormously and spread sideways from universities to community colleges, prep schools, and arts associations. I used to think, "Well, this is nice while it lasts, but it'll go away." It hasn't gone away. There are more than ever.

We were talking about your Paris Review *interviews. You also edited poetry for the* Paris Review *for nine years, at the beginning of the magazine. Why did you want to edit?*

At that time I was a fierce advocate of the contemporary, with huge dislikes and admirations, and I wanted to impose my taste. That's why I did the *Advocate* at Harvard, why I did the *Paris Review,* why I did anthologies. When I was at Oxford, besides choosing poetry for the *Paris Review,* I edited a mimeoed sheet for the Poetry Society, another magazine called *New Poems,* the poetry in the weekly *Isis,* and *Fantasy Poets*—a pamphlet series which was started by a surrealist painter who did printing on the side. Michael Shanks edited the first four *Fantasy* pamphlets—including mine—and when

Shanks went down to London, I chose the second bunch, which included Geoffrey Hill and Thom Gunn. Oxford was a good time—though I felt rather elderly at Oxford. At Harvard I was a year younger than John Ashbery even, but at Oxford I was older than everybody. I'd been through college, while most of them were just out of boarding school. I had fun being dogmatic and bossy. Over at Cambridge, where there hadn't been any poets for years, Thom Gunn turned up writing those wonderful early poems. When we heard him on the BBC, we invited him over to Oxford. My greatest time as an editor was with Geoffrey Hill. Just before the end of my first year at Oxford, he published a poem in *Isis*—a poem he's never reprinted. Meeting him, I asked him casually if he'd submit a manuscript to the *Fantasy* series. Then I came back to the States for the summer; I was in New Hampshire when Geoffrey's manuscript arrived. I couldn't believe my eyes: "Genesis," "God's Little Mountain," "Holy Thursday." Extraordinary! In the middle of the night I woke up dreaming about it; I turned on the light and read it again.

I accepted the manuscript for the pamphlet series. Later I put "Genesis" in the second issue of the *Paris Review*. Geoffrey was twenty years old.

I believe you were known, for a period in the 1960s, as James Dickey's editor or even as his discoverer.

Oh, I was not his discoverer—but I did publish him early. When I was editing for the *Paris Review* I got poems from an address in Atlanta—long, garrulous poems with good touches. After a while I started writing notes, maybe "sorry" on a printed slip, then "thank you," then a letter saying, "I don't like the middle part." Finally he sent a poem I liked and I took it. We began to correspond, and I discovered that he was in advertising. He sent me a fifteen-second radio ad for Coca-Cola, saying, "This is my latest work."

When I was on the poetry board at Wesleyan, he sent us a book, I think at Robert Bly's urging. But we took two other books ahead of him—we could only do two every season—and one of them was going to be James Wright's third book, which he was calling *Amenities of Stone*. These two books crowded James Dickey out, which was a pity because it was *Drowning with Others*—his best work, I still think. Maybe two months later, my phone rang one morning at about seven A.M. It was Willard Lockwood, director of the Wesleyan University Press, saying that Jim Wright had withdrawn his book. Wesleyan was about to go to press; there was no time for the committee to meet again. Would it be all right to substitute the runner-up book, which was James Dickey's? I called Dickey in Atlanta, then and there, seven-thirty in the morning, and asked, "Has your book been taken by another publisher? Can we still have it?" He said to go right ahead. So Wesleyan published James Dickey because James Wright withdrew his book.

Did you get to know James Dickey?

I think I first met him out at Reed College, when he was teaching there for a semester. Poetry got him out of advertising and for a while he traveled from school to school, one year here and another year there. I'm not sure which year he spent at Reed—early sixties—but we had a good visit out there. Carolyn Kizer came down from Seattle. Jim and I drove around in his MG, talking. He was friendly, and flattering about my work, but I began to notice—because of things he said about other people—that loyalty might not be his strong point. So I asked him straight out, "Don't you think loyalty's a great quality?" He knew what I was up to; he said, "No, I think it's a terrible quality. I think it's the worst quality there is."

Let's move away from editing other people to editing yourself. Could you talk about how you work? I gather that you revise a lot.

First drafts of anything are difficult for me. I prefer revising, rewriting. I'm not the kind of writer, like Richard Wilbur or Thomas Mann, who finishes one segment before going onto another. Wilbur finishes the first line before he starts the second. I lack the ability to judge myself except over many drafts, and usually over years. Revising, I go through a whole manuscript over and over and over. Some short prose pieces

I've rewritten fifteen or twenty times; poems get up to two hundred and fifty or three hundred drafts. I don't recommend it—but for me it seems necessary. And I do more drafts as I get older. Or maybe I just like it. Even with prose, I love the late stage in rewriting. I *play* with sentences, revise their organization, work with the rhythms, work with punctuation as though I were handling line-breaks in poetry. In poetry I play with punctuation, line-breaks, internal sounds, interconnections among images. I tinker with little things, and it's my greatest pleasure in writing.

Do you generally have several things going at once?

I'm not good at working on one thing straight through. When I work more than an hour on one subject, I get irritated. Or sometimes I get too high. I spend my day working on many different things, never so long as an hour. When I get stuck, I put it down. Maybe I go haul some wood or have a drink of water; then I come back and pick up something else—an essay I'm working on, a book that's due in six months . . . I work on poems usually in one block of time for a hour or two hours—recently sometimes three hours; things have been hotting up—almost always on several poems.

It isn't just alternating projects; I switch around among genres, and I work in many: children's books, magazine pieces, short stories, textbooks. Obviously I care about poetry the most. But I love working with various kinds of prose also, even something as mundane as headnotes for an anthology. After all, I am working with the same material—language, syntax, rhythms, and vowels—as if I were a sculptor who worked at carving in stone all morning, then in the afternoon built drywalls or fieldstone houses.

There's pleasure in doing the same thing in different forms. When I heard the story of the ox-cart man from my cousin Paul Fenton, I started work on a poem. It's a wonderful story, passed on orally for generations until I stole it out of the air: A farmer fills up his ox cart in October with everything that the farm has produced in a year that he doesn't need—honey, wool, deerskin—and walks by his ox to Portsmouth market where he sells everything in the cart. Then he sells the cart, then the ox, and walks home to start everything over again. The best stories come out of the air. I worked on that oxcart man poem, brief as it is, for about two years.* Just as I was finishing it, I suddenly thought that I could make a children's book out of the same story. The children's book took me a couple of hours to write, hours not years, and the wage was somewhat better. When the book won the Caldecott, we were able to tear off the dingy old bathroom and put a new bathroom into an old bedroom and add a new bedroom; over the new bathroom we have a plaque: CALDECOTT ROOM.

Later I used the same ox-cart story as part of an essay, as a song that Bill Bolcom set for Joan Morris to sing. Now I've used it again, here in an interview! Every time I tell the story it's different. The form makes it different, also the audience and therefore the tone, therefore the diction—which makes the whole process fascinating. In working on a play, I used material from all over the place: from one prose book in particular, from other essays, from fiction, from poems. When I put these things into bodily action, and into dialogue on a stage—material that I had already *used up*, you might have thought—they took on new life, thanks to the collision with a different genre.

You mentioned sculpture a few minutes ago. What is it about Henry Moore that so fascinates you?

I had admired his work for a long time before I had a chance to interview him for *Horizon*. When I was an undergraduate I pinned a Penguin Print of a Henry Moore drawing on my wall. When I first got to England in 1951, I saw his sculpture at the Festival of Britain. It was 1959 when I met him and interviewed him; three years later I came back and hung around him for a whole year—watching, listening—to do a *New Yorker* profile, which later became a book. Of all the older

*One year. My numbers are always unreliable.

artists I've known, he's made the most difference for my own writing. He helped me get past a childish form of ambition: the mere striving to be foremost. He wasn't interested in being the best sculptor in England, or even the best sculptor of his generation. He wanted to be as good as Michelangelo or Donatello. He was in his early sixties when I met him first—my age now—and oh, he loved to work! At the same time he was a gentle, humorous, gregarious man. He got up early every morning—and he *got on with it*. I think of a story from the time when he and Irina were first married. They were going off into the country for a holiday, and Irina tried to lift one of the suitcases that Henry had brought but she couldn't get it off the ground. He'd packed a piece of alabaster. I am sure that they paid lots of attention to each other—but from time to time Henry went outside their tent and tap-tapped with chisel and mallet.

I loved hearing him talk about sculpture, and everything he said about sculpture I turned into poetry. He quoted Rodin quoting a craftsman: "Never think of a surface except as the extension of a volume." I did a lot with that one.

Do you envy him for the physicality of his materials?

The physical activity of the painter and the sculptor keeps them in touch with the *nature* of their art more than writing does for writers. Handwriting or typing or word processing—they're not like sticking your hands into clay.

Yet a poem has a body, just as sculpture and painting have bodies. When you write a poem, you're not hammering out the sounds with a chisel or spreading them with a brush, but you've got to *feel* them in your mouth. The act of writing a poem is a bodily act as well as a mental and imaginative act, and the act of reading a poem—even silently—must be bodily before it's intellectual. In talking or writing about poetry, too often people never get to the work of art. Instead they talk about some statement they abstract from the work of art, a paraphrase of it. Everybody derides paraphrase and everybody does it. It's the fallacy of content—the philosophical heresy.

You were talking about writing prose. Tell us more about the relationship between your poetry and your prose.

When I was young I wrote prose but I didn't take it seriously; it was terrible. I began to write real prose when I wrote *String Too Short to Be Saved,* mostly in 1959 and 1960; with that book I learned how to write descriptive and narrative reminiscence. Over the years, I've learned how to write other prose—to write for five-year-olds, stories for picture books; to write articles or reviews about poetry; to write prose for popular magazines, some of it objective or biographical—like my profile of Henry Moore; and to write about sports. Also I've written short stories, combining narrative prose with some of the shapeliness of poems. Writing prose for a living—freelance writing—does another thing I like: It opens doors. Sir Kenneth Clark had me to lunch at his castle in Kent—because I was writing about Moore for the *New Yorker.* Through sports writing I made the major leagues, talking with Pete Rose and sitting up half the night with Willie Crawford. I've listened to the free association of Kevin McHale of the Boston Celtics.

How did the baseball players accept you? As I remember, when you tried out for the Pirates you were bearded and, shall we say, a touch overweight?

I was bearded and weighed about two hundred fifty pounds when I tried out for second base with the Pittsburgh Pirates. Willie Randolph and Rennie Stennett *both* beat me out. (I was cut for not being able to bend over, which wasn't fair: Richie Hebner made the team at third base and he couldn't bend over either.) The players had nicknames for me, like "Abraham" and "Poet," and they treated me like a mascot. When I took batting practice, the whole team stopped whatever it was doing to watch—the comedy act of the decade. The players looked at me as some sort of respite from their ordinary chores; they were curious, and they were kind enough as they teased me. Mostly, athletes are quick-witted and funny, with maybe a ten-second attention span.

Back to the question: There are several relationships between my prose and my poetry. Prose is mostly the breadwinner. Poetry supplies bread through the poetry reading, but prose makes the steady income. I get paid for an essay once when it comes out in a magazine, then again when I collect it in a book. But also, I think that prose takes some of the pressure off my poetry. Maybe I am able to be more patient with my poetry—taking years and years to finish poems—because I continue to finish and publish short prose pieces.

Prose is tentative and exploratory and not so intense; in prose I can dwell on something longer, not just pick out the *one* thing to notice or say. Poetry is the top of the mountain. I like the foothills just fine—as long as I keep access to the top of the mountain.

Have you ever learned from critics?

Sure. When I was young, critics helped teach me to read poems. Then critics or poets-being-critics have—in person and by letter—led me to discard poems or to rip them up and start over again. I seek their abrasiveness out. I've even been helped by book reviews, mostly by some general dissatisfaction with my work. But if a book review is a personal attack—someone obviously *hates* you—it doesn't do any good. You just walk up and down feeling the burden of this death-ray aimed at you. The critics who help have been annoyed with my work, and made it clear why, without actually wanting to kill me. They give me new occasions for scrutiny, for crossing out.

Another subject. You're notorious for answering letters. Is your heavy correspondence related to your art? Doesn't it get in the way?

Sometimes I wonder: Do I write a letter because it's easier than writing a poem? I don't think so. Letters take less time than parties or lunches. How do people in New York get anything done? My letters are my society. I carry on a dense correspondence with poets of my generation and younger. Letters are my café, my club, my city. I am fond of my neighbors up here, but for the most part they keep as busy as I do. We meet in church, we meet at the store, we gossip a little. We don't stand around in a living room and *chat*—like the parties I used to go to in Ann Arbor. I write letters instead, and mostly I write about the work of writing. There are poets with whom I regularly exchange poems, soliciting criticism. I don't think that either Robert Bly or I has ever published a poem without talking it over with the other. Also, I work out ideas in letters, things that will later be parts of essays. I dictate; it takes too much time to type and no one can read my handwriting.

Let me ask a typical Paris Review *question. Do you write your poems in long hand? On a typewriter? Or a word processor? Do you use a pen? A pencil?*

For thirty or thirty-five years, I've written in long hand— pencil, ballpoint, felt tip, fountain pen: The magic moves around. I used to work at poetry on a typewriter, but I tended to race on, to be glib, not to pause enough. Thirty years ago I gave up the keyboard, began writing in long hand, and hired other people to type for me. At the moment four people help me out, and one right down the road has a word processor. It's marvelous because I can tinker without worrying about the time and labor of retyping. I make little changes in ongoing poems every day, and start with clean copies every morning.

I dictate letters but nothing else. It irritates me that Henry James was able to dictate *The Ambassadors* but I can't dictate the first draft of a book review.

Were you ever part of a group of poets? Did you visit Robert Bly's farm in the early sixties in Madison, Minnesota?

There wasn't anything I would call a group—though earlier I guess I spoke of "my gang." I did get out to Robert and Carol Bly's a couple of times. The summer of 1961 I was there for two weeks along with the Simpsons. Jim Wright came out from Minneapolis for the two weekends. We four males spent hours together looking at each other's poetry. Of course we had some notions in common, and we learned from each other, so maybe we *were* a group. Or at least a "gang." I remember how one poem of mine got changed then, "In the Kitchen of the Old House." I'd been fiddling with it for two years. It began with an imagined dream—which just didn't go—and I said in frustration something like, "I remember when this started. I was sitting in the kitchen of this old house late at night, thinking about . . ." Three voices interrupted me: "Write it down! Write it down!" This poem needed a way *in*.

We worked together and we played competitive games like badminton and swimming, but poetry was the most competitive game. We were friendly and fought like hell. Louis was the best swimmer, and Robert always won the foolhardiness prize. There was a big town swimming pool in Madison where we went every day, and Robert would climb to the highest diving platform and jump off, making faces and noises and gyrating his body all the way down. I won at badminton.

Robert and I—he was Bob then; I feel stiff saying "Robert"—met at Harvard in February of 1948, when I tried out for the *Advocate*. He had joined the previous fall, when he first got to Harvard, but I waited until my second term. After school was out that summer, he came down to Connecticut and stayed at my house for a day or two. I was nervous having my poet friend there, afraid of confrontation between Robert and my father. At lunch Robert said, "Well, Mr. Hall, what do you think of having a poet for a son?" As I feared, my father didn't know *what* to say; poetry was embarrassing, somehow. So I said, "Too bad your father doesn't have the same problem," and my father laughed and laughed, off the hook.

Robert and I have written thousands of letters back and forth, and we've visited whenever we could. You know these people who hate Robert and write about how clever he has been at his literary politicking? They don't know anything about it. For years and years he was a solitary. I remember a time before I moved to Ann Arbor, when Robert came back from Norway and stopped to visit while I lived outside Boston. He was talking about going back to the Madison farm and starting a magazine. He had discovered international modernism in Norway and wanted to *tell* everybody—but also he wanted to remain independent. Having literary friends would only make it harder for him, so he did not want to *know* anybody besides me. Then he said, "I don't want to know James Wright. How can I write about James Wright if I know James Wright?" He wasn't being nasty about Jim; he brought up Jim's name because Jim had just taken a job at the University of Minnesota—three or four hours away from Madison. They didn't get to know each other until a couple of years later, when Jim wrote him an anguished letter. Jim read Robert's attacks on fifties poetry in *The Fifties* and decided that everything Robert said was right and everything Jim was doing was wrong. Jim was always deciding that he was *wrong*.

Robert wanted solitude and independence. He was going to lecture everybody, as he always has done and still does, but from a distance. If he wanted eminence he wanted a lonely eminence. He came out of his isolation, I think, at that conference in Texas when he took the floor away from the professors. Do you know about that?

No. This is something I haven't heard about.

It was a moment. The National Council of Teachers of English invited young poets, as they called us, to a conference in Houston in 1966. They brought Robert Graves over to lecture, and they brought in Richard Eberhart, calling him dean of the younger poets. Dick was fifty-two; that made him dean. Most of the young poets were forty or close to it. There was W. S. Merwin, Robert Creeley, Robert Duncan, Gary Snyder, Carolyn Kizer, Robert, and I . . . And also: Reed Whittemore, Josephine Miles, William Stafford, May Swenson. Young poets! Several of us flew down from Chicago together. We stood in the aisle of a 707 singing "Yellow Submarine"—Bly, Snyder, Creeley, and I. We stayed up all night in somebody's room at the Houston hotel talking about poetry. Creeley had an over-the-shoulder cassette recorder, and every time Duncan spoke he turned it on, and every time Duncan finished speaking he turned it off. We stayed up until six in the morning and Eberhart's talk was at eight-thirty, so we didn't get a whole lot of sleep.

We met in a huge hall filled with hundreds and hundreds

of English teachers. Eberhart talked about how the Peace Corps sent him to Africa; he observed a tribe of primitive people and told us that civilization lacked spontaneity. Dick discovers Rousseau! Someone else got up, a respondent, and said something silly. Then Lawrence Perrine, who edited the textbook *Sound and Sense,* stood up as another respondent. He talked conservatively about poetic form, saying something in praise of villanelles—in 1966!—which made it sound as if all poems were really the same; as if nothing mattered, not what you said or how you said it. I'm unfair, but all of us were tired, some of us were hung over, and everything we heard sounded fatuous after the energizing talk of the night before. So Robert stood up in the front row—turning around to face these crowds of people, interrupting the program—and said: "He's *wrong.* We care about poetry. Poetry *matters* and one thing is better than something else . . ." He went on; I can't remember . . . Whatever Bly said, it was passionate. It woke everybody up, I'll tell you. A thousand teachers applauded mightily. As Robert sat down the program was about to proceed, and somebody in the audience called out: "Let's hear from all the poets." So we took over, to hell with the program, and one by one each of us read a poem and talked. It was Vietnam time and a lot of us talked about politics. Robert gave the rest of us courage, and his platform life began at that moment: He had found his public antinomian *presence.*

Somehow one doesn't think of Robert Bly as having graduated from Harvard—but there were many poets there at the time, weren't there?

Robert went one year to St. Olaf in Minnesota and then transferred to Harvard. He and I overlapped for three years, becoming closest friends, always opposites. The two of us are Don Quixote and Sancho Panza. On the *Advocate* with us were Kenneth Koch and John Ashbery. Frank O'Hara was never on the *Advocate,* but he was a member of the first class I took in writing, taught by John Ciardi, who was a wonderful teacher. I remember John coming into class one day and saying something like, "I just sold eight poems to the *New Yorker,* I bought my first car, and next election I'll probably vote Republican."

John supported Henry Wallace in 1948, very progressive. Be wary of what you joke about. O'Hara was writing poems then, but I didn't know it; I saw his short stories. Frank gave the best parties at Harvard: incongruous, outrageous bunches of people. I remember Maurice Bowra, visiting from Oxford, as he bounced and burbled on Frank's sofa. Frank was in Eliot House, as I was, and his roommate was the artist Ted Gorey—Edward St. John Gorey. Frank was the funniest man I ever met, utterly quick-witted and sharp with his sarcasm. Once in his presence I made some sort of joshing reference, comparing him to Oscar Wilde. Being gay was relatively open, even light, in the Harvard of those years. One of Frank's *givens* was that *everybody* was gay, either in or out of the closet. He answered me with a swoop of emphasis: *"You're* the type that would *sue."*

I admired Ashbery; we *all* admired John, although in general we were not a mutual admiration society. (In general we were murderous.) John was at that time reticent, shy, precocious. He had published in *Poetry* while he was still at Deerfield Academy. On the *Advocate,* we were terribly serious about the poems we published. We would stay up until two or three in the morning arguing about whether a poem was good enough to be in the magazine. One time we had a half-page gap and asked John to come up with a poem. After some prodding, he conceded that *maybe* he had a poem. He went back to his room to get it, and it took him forty minutes. We didn't know it then, but of course—he later admitted—he went home and wrote the poem. In 1989 I told John this story—wondering if he remembered it as I did—and he even remembered the *poem,* which began, "Fortunate Alphonse, the shy homosexual . . ." He told me, with a sigh, "Yes, I took longer then."

One night Bly came back from a dance at Radcliffe saying he had met a girl from Baltimore, a doctor's daughter who knew all about modern poetry. Adrienne Rich! I met her and we dated, though we didn't get to know each other until a couple of years later. She published her first book, which Auden chose for the Yale Series of Younger Poets, when we were seniors. My second year at Oxford, she won a Guggenheim (at the age of twenty-two) and chose to spend her time in Oxford—not studying, just in town. That's when we became friends, and for several years we worked closely together. In 1954 and 1955 Adrienne and I were back in Cambridge at the same time. I baby-sat every morning while my wife went back to school, and one day a week Adrienne, pregnant with her first child, dropped by from eight in the morning until one o'clock. We talked poetry while I fed and bathed my son Andrew. Many years later, Adrienne and I were talking about those times, early marriages and casserole cookery, and we talked about the sex roles we played. "Don," Adrienne told me, "you taught me how to bathe a baby."

At Harvard, I also knew Peter Davison, L. E. Sissman, Kenward Elmslie. Bob Creeley left the term before I arrived. He was chicken farming in New Hampshire but I met him and talked poetry with him at the Grolier Book Shop, where you met everybody. Creeley and I got along famously, but a couple of years later I insulted him in a magazine piece and we were enemies for a while. A little while ago, Bob sent me a book that included a stick figure account of his life, and he put a check mark by one item: He had quit a publishing venture, on Majorca with Martin Seymour-Smith, because Seymour-Smith wanted to print my poems.

Richard Wilbur was older—he was born in 1921, and at that time, seven years difference was something. While I was an undergraduate, he was a junior fellow, with a young family at home, so he had a room at Adams House to work in. He was such a generous man. I brought him poems to look at, and he showed me what he was up to. I remember him working on *Ceremony*. Archibald MacLeish came to Harvard as Boylston Professor when I was a junior. Dick Eberhart lived in Cambridge. Frost lived there fall and spring, and when I was a junior fellow Robert Lowell came to Boston. Quite a bunch.

Did you know Lowell?

A little. *Lord Weary's Castle* was my favorite book of the time—which it still is—and I loved "Mother Marie Therese" and "Falling Asleep Over the Aeneid" from the next book. When the *Life Studies* poems started in magazines, a little later, it was totally shocking; but some were great. I can't remember how we met. He and Elizabeth Hardwick came to dinner and we went to their place. There was a bunch that met for a workshop a few times at John Holmes's house—Phil Booth and Lowell and Holmes and me. Lowell was gentle and soft-spoken—I never saw him when he was in trouble—but candid. These get-togethers were fine, but they never flew. Maybe I was too much in awe. For a while Lowell wrote me some of those postcards he was famous for. He wrote about an essay I did in which I said that every time I learned to make a new noise in poetry I found something new to say. He said he'd heard me say the same thing at a Harvard reading, and that it helped him toward *Life Studies*. A few years later, out in Ann Arbor, he came to my house and we spent an evening together drinking and reading poems out loud. He read me most of *Near the Ocean*. I was surprised by how much he wanted my approval—but of course, like anybody, he wanted *everybody's*. Then when he started doing self-imitations with the *Notebook* stuff, I was disappointed. Hell, I was furious—he let me down, as it were—and I attacked him in print. He quoted from one of my attacks in a later notebook-poem—and he rewrote my words a little, so that they sounded more pompous—but he didn't say whom he quoted. We never saw each other after that.

After your time at Oxford, you spent a year at Stanford studying with Yvor Winters, whose name is not generally associated with yours. What came out of that experience?

I learned more about poetry in a year, working with Winters, than I did in the rest of my education. Also, I was fond of him—we even stayed in his house during Christmas vacation while he went off to visit relatives—but one incident in the spring gave me pause. At a party at his house, he said to me, "Would you get some more ice, son?" When he called me son it was as if he breathed in my ear; I'd follow him anywhere. I thought: *It's good I'm getting out of here.*

When I went to Stanford, I had already spent years working in a conservative poetic. In those days, most of us worked in a rhymed iambic line. I did it—and James Wright, Louis Simpson, Galway Kinnell, Adrienne Rich, Robert Bly, W. D. Snodgrass, W. S. Merwin. When I applied for the fellowship, my work didn't depart greatly from the structure and metrics that Winters advocated. He thought I had some technical competence, or I wouldn't have had the fellowship. The best poem I wrote at Stanford was "My Son, My Executioner," which could almost have come out of the seventeenth century—the abstract diction, the way it looks reasonable treating the irrational. For that one year I became briefly more conservative than ever, and it became known that I was the poetry editor for the *Paris Review.* Some old acquaintances sent me poems, including Frank O'Hara. Frank hadn't discovered himself, quite—but he wasn't writing rhymed iambic pentameter either. I rejected his poems and wrote a supercilious note. Stupid! Not long ago I came across Frank's answer, in which he accused me of writing second-rate Yeats, which was perfectly true. The letter is snippy, funny, outraged, but *cool.*

I regret I didn't have the brains to take his poems, but I couldn't read them then. I *did* do early work by Hill, Gunn, Bly, Simpson, Wright, Rich, Merwin . . . lots of people. But, also I rejected a good poem by Allen Ginsberg, who wrote George Plimpton saying that I wouldn't recognize a poem if it buggered me in broad daylight.

Back to the way you write. Has it changed over the years?

When I was younger, poems arrived in a rush, maybe six or eight new things begun in two days, four days. I'd be in a crazy mood, inspired; I'd walk into furniture and not recognize my children. After the initial bursts, I would have my task set out before me—to bring out what was best, to get rid of the bad stuff, to work them over until I was pleased or satisfied. Then, for nine years or so—late thirties into forties—I was unable to write anything that was up to what I'd done earlier. I thought I'd lost it. After all, if you read biography, you know: *People lose it.* Then in the autumn of 1974 I started

Kicking the Leaves, and most people think that's when I finally got started as a poet. I was forty-six.

With these new poems, I began to follow a different process of composition, one I've stuck with ever since. Usually now I begin with a loose association of images, a scene, and a sense that somewhere in this material is something I don't yet understand that *wants* to become a poem. I write out first drafts in prosaic language—flat, no excitement. Then very slowly, over dozens or even hundreds of drafts, I begin to discover and exploit connections—between words, between images. Looking at a poem on the five-hundredth day, I will take one word out and put in another. Three days later I will discover that the new word connects with another word that joined the manuscript a year back.

Now inspiration doesn't come at once, several poems starting in a few days; it comes in the discovery of a single word after three years of work. This process never stops. When a new book of mine arrives in the mail, I dread reading it—because I know I will find words I want to change. I revise when I read my poems out loud to an audience. I change them when they appear in magazines or anthologies. I can't keep my hands off my poems. I wrote "The Man in the Dead Machine" in 1965, published it in 1966, and read it aloud a thousand times. Then in April of 1984, driving to Scranton airport after a reading, I saw how to make it better. So I did.

The kind of poem I've taken to writing is something you could call the discursive ode. I call it an ode because although it's lyrical it tries for a certain length and inclusiveness. I call it discursive because it appears to wander, to move from one particular to another by association, though if it succeeds it finds a unity. It tries to connect things difficult to connect, things that at first seem diverse; often the images make a structural glue. I suppose it's largely a romantic form but one can find classical sources for it, in Latin satire, maybe in some of Horace's odes, maybe even in neoclassic poems by Johnson and Pope. But it flowers in the ode, even in something as short as the "Ode to a Nightingale" or later "Among School Children."

You seemed, with Kicking the Leaves, *to enter a third phase of your career. Somewhere, in an essay or interview, I believe you described the first two phases. In the first, you wrote a poetry of the top of the mind, where consciousness was very much in control. In the second phase, you reversed that, letting the unconscious mind rule, letting all sorts of unexpected and unsettling things into the poem. Now in the third phase it may be that you are combining the two.*

That's a goal. Even when I was in the second phase, dredging things from the dark places, I wanted to bring them into the light. Freud said, "Where Id was, let there Ego be." I wanted to subject things—even subterranean things—to the light of consciousness. During the first phase, I had a dream of conscious control, *libido sciendi;* unconscious materials only occurred when I hid them from myself, as in "The Sleeping Giant," where I wrote an Oedipal poem without any idea of what I was doing. Today when I begin writing I'm aware: *Something that I don't understand drives this engine.* Why do I pick *this* scene or image? Within the action of kicking the leaves something was weighted, freighted, heavy with feeling—and because I kept writing, kept going back to the poem, eventually the under-feeling that unified the detail came forward in the poem. The process is discovered by revision, uncovering by persistence.

Was your recent long poem, The One Day, *written in this way?*

This material started to arrive during my years of flailing about. It came in great volcanic eruptions of language. I couldn't drive to the supermarket without taking a note pad with me. I kept accumulating fragments without reading them or rewriting; it was as if I was finding the stone that I would eventually carve a sculpture from. Then when it stopped coming, I went back and read it. It was chaotic, full of inadequate language—and it was also scary. There was spooky stuff out of childhood; there was denunciation and mockery that years later went into "Prophecy" and "Pastoral." Something let me loose into this material, something that I was scared to revisit. So I let it rest, waiting until the lava cooled down and hardened. That took years. Finally, in 1979 or 1980, I took a deep breath and began to try to make it into poetry. And I added new material; half of the poem—or more—came during the later writing. There were false starts; at one point, maybe in 1982, I had a long asymmetric free verse poem in thirty or forty sections, each several pages long and with its own title. No good. Later I discovered the ten-line blocks that I could build with. I could keep them discrete or I could bridge from one to the next.

When you describe your process of discovery, in conversation, you seem almost to be describing the process of free association that a psychoanalyst asks for. Is this parallel valid?

It's no accident. I spent seven years in therapy, up to three times a week, with a Freudian analyst. He was an old man with a light Austrian accent and athletic eyebrows; I would explain, carefully and reasonably, why I had done something cruel or stupid; his eyebrows would do the high jump. We fell into the habit of treating poems as dreams. When you bring a dream to a therapist or analyst, he or she isn't likely to pay attention to the manifest content, but if you have a table in that dream he may ask, "What does the table look like?" The table might be the key to what the dream—or poem—is actually about. In "The Alligator Bride" there's an Empire table. Freudian analysis is a word cure, and it resembles the way we read or write poems. Poems that I wrote in my frenzy were *like* dreams, because they allowed something unconscious to loosen forth. Those years allowed me to overcome fears of hidden things and let them out. Coming into my doctor's office, I learned how to tap instantly into the on-flowing current inside my head. That essential step took me about a year, but once you learn it you don't lose it. I learned to listen for the vatic voice, to watch images running over the mindscreen, to give a telegraphic account of what I heard and saw. It was good for me as a creature and good for me as a poet. Even now I talk with my doctor every day of my life and he explains the sources of feeling—although he's dead. Eventually it was psychotherapy that allowed me to recover my life. And to write *The One Day*.

So there is a sense in which you are touching a deeper Donald Hall in this material.

I hope so, yes. Not in any boring autobiographical way. In *The Happy Man* I have a poem in which somebody talks about his time in the detox center. A friend asked me what I was in detox for. Well, I never was. For the poem I made up a character; I talked through a mask I invented, which I do all the time. I love to fool people, even with fake epigraphs—but also I wish they weren't fooled. Of course my poems use things that have happened to me—but they go beyond the facts. Even when I write about my grandfather, I lie. I don't believe poets when they say "I," and I wish people wouldn't believe me. Poetic material starts by being personal but the deeper we go inside the more we become everybody.

Has the passage of time, the coming of age, if you will, caused any other changes in your notions about your poetry, your career as a poet?

I'm more patient now. When I was in my twenties, I wanted to write many poems. I had goals; when I reached them, they turned out to be not worth reaching. When you begin, you think that if you could just publish a few poems, you'd reach your desire; then if you could publish in a good magazine; then if you could publish a book; then . . . When you've done these things you haven't done anything. The desire must be, not to write another dozen poems, but to write something as good as the poems that originally brought you to love the art. It's the only sensible reason for writing poems. You've got to keep your eye on what you care about: To write a poem that stands with Walt Whitman or Andrew Marvell.

Another thing that's changed is my sense of daily time. I spent years of my life daydreaming about a future, I suppose in order to avoid a present that was painful. Teaching in Ann Arbor I daydreamed about a year in England. Mentally I lived always a step ahead of myself, so that the day I lived in was something to get through, on the way to something else. Pitiful! After I left teaching, when Jane and I had lived at Eagle Pond for a year, I realized: I'm aware of the hour I live in; I'm not daydreaming ahead to a future time; I know which direction the wind blows from, and where the sun is; I'm alive in the present moment, in what I do *now*, and in where I'm doing it. This present includes layers of the past—there's so much past at Eagle Pond—but it doesn't depend on a daydream future that may never arrive.

You've always written a lot about Eagle Pond, things like how your grandmother used to stand at the kitchen window in the morning and check the mountain. Well, it's the same window today and the same mountain. The profound presence of the past in a place like this, even the felt presence of those who have lived here but are now dead, the cows and other animals in your poems—does all this have anything to do with the general elegiac cast to your poetry?

My grandmother's father, who was born in 1826 and who died fifteen years before I was born, looked out that same window to check that same mountain. I stand in the footprints of people long gone—which I find an inspiriting connection; it belittles the notion of one's own death; it says: "That's all right. Everybody who has looked at this mountain has died or will die. *Then others will look at it.*" A sense of continuity makes for an elegiac poetry. One of my first published poems, when I was sixteen, was about a New Hampshire graveyard. When we were at Harvard, Robert Bly used to call me the cellar-hole poet—like a graveyard poet in the eighteenth century. When I spent my childhood summers here, among the old people, *absence* was everywhere. Walking in the woods I found cellar holes, old wells, old walls. Even now you can sometimes feel under your feet, in dense woods, the ruts that plows made long ago.

As you talk about this, I hear almost a sacred sense of place. You have written about attending church here as primarily a social experience—but you are also a deacon, and I am wondering about the more serious implications of this activity.

It began from a social feeling, but moved on—from community to communion. When I was a child I went to church every Sunday simply because that was what we did. Uncle Luther, my grandmother's older brother, who grew up in this house, was our preacher. He'd retired from a Connecticut parish and at eighty delivered lucid fifteen-minute sermons without a note in front of him. He was born in 1856 and could remember the Civil War. I used to sit on the porch and get him to tell me stories about the Civil War.

I enjoyed church as a child—sitting beside my grandfather, all dressed up, who fed me Canada mints. But I can't say that I was taken with Christian thought or theology. When I was about twelve I had the atheist experience. I suddenly realized, with absolute clarity, that there was no God. With this knowledge, I felt superior to other people. Twenty years later, when I was living in an English village called Thaxted, I fell into the habit of attending church every Sunday, I *thought* without religious feeling; I loved the ceremony, and the wonderful old communist vicar, Jack Putterill. His church used a pre-prayer-book service that was so high only dogs could hear it, and his sermon, after incense and holy water, was a fifteen-minute communist homily. I thought I attended these services out of aesthetic and social motives; now I suspect that I harbored religious feelings I feared to acknowledge.

In Ann Arbor I never went to church. When Jane and I moved back here, I must have been ready. On that first Sunday, I thought, "They will expect us to go to church." We decided to go just that once. In the middle of his sermon, our minister quoted Rilke. I'd never heard Rilke quoted in the South Danbury Church! We were already fond of the people—mostly cousins—and we went back next Sunday, and the next. Slowly, we started reading the Gospels, and some Christian thought—like "The Cloud of Unknowing," Meister Eckhart, Julian of Norwich. At one point that winter Jane was sick and couldn't go. I said, "I'll stay home with you." Five minutes before church, I said, "I can't stand it," and off I went. These feelings amazed me . . . and they were accompanied by thoughts: Our minister ranged all over the place in his sermons. He loved Dietrich Bonhoeffer, the German Protestant theologian who plotted against Hitler and was executed, a modern saint and martyr.

By this time, I would like to call myself a Christian, though I feel shy about it. We have many visitors whom Christianity makes nervous; they seem *embarrassed* for us. So many people expend their spirituality piecemeal on old superstitions like astrology that they entertain but don't believe in—like the imperial Romans and their gods. I dislike contemporary polytheism, that nervous searching that provides itself with so many alternatives that it doesn't stick itself with belief: the God-of-the-Month Club.

The minister who loved Bonhoeffer and mentioned Rilke was Jack Jensen, who died of cancer in 1990. We feel terrible grief over him. He taught at Colby-Sawyer College, nearby, and had a divinity degree from Yale as well as a Ph.D. in philosophy from Boston University, a man of spirit and brains together. Watching him, listening to him, I became aware that it was possible to be a Christian although subject to skepticism and spiritual dryness. I used to think that Christians believed *everything,* and *all the time,* which is nonsense. If you have no dry spells, I doubt your spirit. We watched Jack live through the deserts, when he would give sermons that were historical or philosophical. After a while he would liven up, go spiritually green again. He was a great one for Advent, the annual birth or rebirth of everything possible. Although the history of the church is often horrible—I always think of Servetus, the Spanish humanist condemned to the stake by the Italian Inquisition, who escaped to Geneva, where Calvin's people burned him—still, there's power in two thousand years of worship and ritual coded into our Sundays. In China we went to an Easter service and heard the choir belt out "Up from the Grave He Arose" in Chinese. So much culture and geography collapse into the figure of Christ. That's what remains, after all, at the bottom of the two thousand years—this extraordinary figure in Palestine, the figure of Christ.

I haven't asked you about Jane Kenyon. There are after all two poets of Eagle Pond Farm.

I know. Everything that my life has come to—coming here, the church, my poems of the last fifteen years—derives from my marriage to Jane in 1972. And I've watched her grow into a *poet*. Amazing. Of course we work together, show each other what we're doing, occasionally getting a little huffy with each other but helping each other all the same. But it's living with her that's made all the difference for me. We have the church together as well as the poetry and baseball. But I don't want to go on about it. I don't want to sound like someone making an acknowledgment in a book. Someday she'll do her own *Paris Review* interview.

Let's end with one more historical question. Since we are talking just now on the stage at the Y in New York City, I wonder if you would tell me the story of the first reading you gave here.

I think it was in 1956, thirty-four years ago, that I read here for the first time. I was on a program with May Swenson and Alastair Reid, and I read third. In those days, instead of all three of us sitting out here and listening to each other, we waited in the green room until it was our turn. I was nervous. This reading might have been my second or third ever, certainly my first in New York City—and this was the Y. I nipped at the scotch that Betty Kray provided in the green room. Then I thought about where I was and I nipped some more. When I came out here to read, I was still able to see the pages of my book, and I didn't fall down, but I was horrible. I was at a stage of drunkenness that allowed me to think I was George Sanders. I felt wonderful sophistication and coolness, sure that everything I said was utterly witty and wonderful. I was a horse's ass.

journal. "Goldfish are inherently skeptical & their eyes 'look on me with such
as may be the thickness of their glass bowls. (ms60)
I have found so many of them deep me (truly?) (ms60)
None of them believed really do it.

This seems to be a learning-exercise; the problem with the ungrateful beasts seems
was always the most-personal abstraction; skeptical & irrelevant-
Now you have given that skepticism a purpose reason, by telling
The toilet bowl & getting rid of the shake, & toothbrush. Then read the
creepy-ness of an Edison baby carton.

Let's face facts. When I've writed as badly from my first drunk
with marijuana & wine up realizing how sad quickly never
unit poetry. I would have to configure crawford and crazy
up though the stations of the sidewalks crew & pedestant
up that were my certains because I had to often
township. Were my certains came a day & struck off the
secret garments. Slowly came a day & still within cold, chill off an
stations and the crowd. I still struggling with this
repaired. I'm struggling with this
Write two unfinished sonnets.

[ms60] writing one's own novelette.
No thing in the inside world stays secure

UNDER DISCUSSION
Donald Hall, General Editor

Volumes in the Under Discussion series collect reviews and essays about individual poets. The series is concerned with contemporary American and English poets about whom the consensus has not yet been formed and the final vote has not been taken. Titles in the series include:

Elizabeth Bishop and Her Art
edited by Lloyd Schwartz and Sybil P. Estess
Richard Wilbur's Creation
edited and with an Introduction by Wendy Salinger
Reading Adrienne Rich
edited by Jane Roberta Cooper
On the Poetry of Allen Ginsberg
edited by Lewis Hyde
Robert Creeley's Life and Work
edited by John Wilson
On the Poetry of Galway Kinnell
edited by Howard Nelson
On Louis Simpson
edited by Hank Lazer
Anne Sexton
edited by Steven E. Colburn
James Wright
edited by Peter Stitt and Frank Graziano
Frank O'Hara
edited by Jim Elledge
On the Poetry of Philip Levine
edited by Christopher Buckley
The Poetry of W. D. Snodgrass
edited by Stephen Haven
Denise Levertov
edited by Albert Gelpi
On William Stafford
edited by Tom Andrews

Please write for further information on available editions and current prices.